Common Errors in English

David Jowitt MA
Silas Nnamonu MA

Addison Wesley Longman Limited
Edinburgh Gate, Harlow,
Essex CM20 2JE,
England
and associated companies
throughout the world.

First published 1985
Ninth impression 1998
© Longman Group Ltd 1985

Set in Plantin (Linotron 202)

Produced by Addison Wesley Longman China Limited, Hong Kong.
NPCC/09

ISBN 0-582-60991-7

Contents

Preface

Common Errors in English is designed for use in Africa by those who can already speak and write English competently enough, but have a persistent tendency to commit certain errors. Some of these violate elementary rules of grammar; others are matters of more advanced lexis and style. Whether elementary or not, very many of them have become so much part of the automatic speech and writing patterns of users of English in Africa, including even highly educated people, that their inclusion here will come as a surprise. Unfortunately, the example set by the highly educated reinforces the tendency for the errors to be acquired by less educated learners, and thus they become seemingly permanent and unassailable, like ants in the kitchen. It goes without saying that inadequate grasp of the rules of English grammar is their general cause, but no doubt the interference of African language patterns also accounts for many of them.

The rules laid down by the book are 'Standard English'. But in many cases the authors were in a dilemma, whether to include as an error a certain form or expression on the simple grounds that it deviates from Standard English; or whether to recognize that certain deviations from Standard English have become so firmly established in this or that part of Africa that to pillory them here would seem fastidious and uncharitable. In the absence of any consensus about the status of 'Nigerian English' or 'East African English' the dilemma remains. However, the authors have partially overcome it by disregarding a number of common lexical deviations from Standard English, even though these cannot be said to have achieved formal acceptance in the countries where they are used.

One obvious result of committing errors is that students may not do as well in public examinations as they expect. But even when the speaker or writer of English has put English examinations behind him he may still, because of his inaccurate use of the language, fail to communicate effectively; and if his otherwise fluent and accurate speech or writing is marred by the errors of a novice, his image as a user of the English may be adversely affected. There is of course a view quite fashionable nowadays that 'mechanical accuracy' does not matter much, that range of vocabulary, expressiveness, and so on, are far more important to the language learner. One reply to this challenge is that to encourage the language user to cultivate the habit of detecting and avoiding incorrect forms is one way of encouraging him to make accuracy and precision of expression in general one of his standards, and that the careful use of language is one of the prerequisites for successful communication at all levels. This book will at any rate prove very helpful, not only in the upper forms of African secondary schools and in tertiary institutions, but also to anyone in Africa who uses English regularly or as a prime means of communication – the teacher, the civil servant, the businessman, the trader, the nurse.

The book examines altogether 650 errors, set out in Chapters 1 to 15. Each chapter deals with errors that commonly occur in the context of a particular word-class (nouns, adjectives, etc.). This arrangement has its drawbacks, but it seemed the best one to follow in the interests of achieving clarity of organization. Within each chapter items are grouped in sections according to the type of error committed, for example 'Singular and Plural Forms Confused'. Full section references are given in the Table of Contents, but the student who has certain words in mind which he wishes to check is advised to look them up in the Index at the back. Each chapter begins with some grammatical explanation, but the authors have tried to keep this to a minimum, and do not pretend to have covered all aspects of the rules enunciated, or all exceptions to them. From time to time the student is referred to Chapter 16, entitled 'Notes on Grammar', where more substantial explanations of selected topics are given. Finally, at the end of the book there are a number of exercises for practice. These are based on the general rules which have been stated in the text, or which the reader is expected already to know; they are therefore designed to assist the learning of correct forms.

The book can be used in various ways by teachers and students working together in the classroom or lecture-hall, or by the general reader or student working on his own.

D.R.J.
S.C.N.

1 Nouns

Every language contains nouns. They refer to people or to things, both concrete (*teacher, farm*) and abstract (*unity, happiness*). A noun can refer to one item (SINGULAR) or to many (PLURAL). Other ways of categorizing nouns are into COMMON and PROPER nouns, and into COUNTABLE and UNCOUNTABLE nouns. More is said about these below, and also on pages 198–9, 201–2, and 220–22.

Incorrect Plurals

The plural of most nouns in English is formed by adding -*s* or -*es* to the singular form. There are special rules for nouns ending in -*y* and for nouns ending in -*f* or -*fe*, and there are a few irregular plurals such as *men, women, children*, etc. Users of this book are expected to be able already to form the plural of any noun correctly.

However, errors sometimes occur with nouns of the -*f* or -*fe* group, since in some cases the *f* changes to *v* and in other cases not. For example:

1 Life
Wrong: Many lifes are lost through road accidents.
Correct: Many lives are lost through road accidents.

A list of irregular plurals appears on pages 218–20.

Wrong addition of '-s' to Uncountable Nouns

Nouns can be classified into those that are COUNTABLE and those that are UNCOUNTABLE. Countable nouns, the majority, can form a plural by adding -*s*. Uncountable nouns cannot take -*s*.

Failure to observe the difference accounts for many common errors.

2 Accommodation
Wrong: They wanted to find some suitable accommodations.

Correct: They wanted to find some suitable accommodation.

3 Advice
Wrong: Fathers are expected to give advices to their sons.

Correct: Fathers are expected to give advice to their sons.

'Advice' in the normal sense of 'counsel' has no plural form in -s; but see also number 81.

4 Ammunition
Wrong: The soldiers had insufficient guns and ammunitions.

Correct: The soldiers had insufficient guns and ammunition.

5 Artillery
Wrong: The general moved up his heavy artilleries.

Correct: The general moved up his heavy artillery.

6 Behaviour
Wrong: They didn't visit anybody at home; I was shocked by their behaviours.

Correct: They didn't visit anybody at home; I was shocked by their behaviour.

The plural 'behaviours' is sometimes found in the very specialized context of academic psychology.

7 Blame
Wrong: Sefi received blames from many people because of her attitude.

Correct: Sefi received blame from many people because of her attitude.

This word can of course take -*s* if it is used as a verb.

8 Chalk

Wrong: The table was covered with chalks.
Correct: The table was covered with chalk *or* with pieces of chalk.

Wrong: There are many chalks in this cupboard.
Correct: There is a lot of chalk in this cupboard.

'Chalks' is correct if it means 'different types', 'different colours' of chalk.

9 Cutlery

Wrong: The cooks never provide enough cutleries.
Correct: The cooks never provide enough cutlery.

10 Dust

Wrong: They could not see because the air was full of dusts.
Correct: They could not see because the air was full of dust.

11 Élite

Wrong: He was one of the élites of his country.
Correct: He belonged to the *or* He was among the élite of his country.

'Élite' means 'select group'; an élite is not an individual person. Also see number 613.

12 Equipment

Wrong: The laboratory contained many different equipments.
Correct: The laboratory contained many different types of equipment *or* a lot of different equipment.

13 Fun

Wrong: They like having a time for funs and riddles during parties.
Correct: They like having a time for jokes and riddles during parties.

As 'fun' cannot be used in the plural, say 'jokes' if plays on words, puzzles, etc. are meant.

14 Furniture
Wrong: Many furnitures are on display in the department store.

Correct: A lot of furniture is *or* Many types of furniture are on display in the department store.

15 Information
Wrong: The latest informations will appear on the board shortly.

Correct: The latest information will appear on the board shortly.

16 Intelligentsia
Wrong: We look to the intelligentsias of the nation for fresh ideas.

Correct: We look to the intelligentsia of the nation for fresh ideas.

17 Jewelry, jewellery (alternative spellings).
Wrong: The robbers took away some precious jewelleries.

Correct: The robbers took away some precious jewellery *or* some precious jewels.

18 Luggage
Wrong: The customs men checked all his luggages very carefully.

Correct: The customs men checked all his luggage *or* all his items of luggage very carefully.

19 Machinery
Wrong: The latest machineries have been installed in the factory.

Correct: The latest machinery has *or* The latest machines have been installed in the factory.

20 Mail
Wrong: The Messenger reported that some mails had been opened.

Correct: The Messenger reported that some of the mail had been opened.

'Mail' means a collection (usually a bag) of letters for posting.

21 Personnel
Wrong: You should apply – the company needs more personnels.

Correct: You should apply – the company needs more personnel.

22 Scenery
Wrong: He observed many beautiful sceneries on his tour of Kenya.

Correct: He observed much beautiful scenery on his tour of Kenya.

23 Slang
Wrong: He speaks his mother tongue well, but uses many slangs.

Correct: He speaks his mother tongue well, but uses a lot of slang.

24 Staff
Wrong: All staffs are expected to be present at the meeting.

Correct: All staff *or* All members of staff are expected to be present at the meeting.

'Staff' is uncountable when it has this meaning, countable when it means 'stick symbolizing authority'.

25 Stationery
Wrong: I must go out and buy some more stationeries.
Correct: I must go out and buy some more stationery.

'Stationery' here means an assorted mass of stationery – letters, envelopes, and so on. The plural form 'stationeries', meaning 'different items of stationery' can be used in a very formal context like accounting, but not in general conversation. Also see number 583.

26 Underwear

Wrong: We have just received a fresh consignment of underwears.

Correct: We have just received a fresh consignment of underwear.

27 Washing

Wrong: His washings had been hanging out to dry for several days.

Correct: His washing had been hanging out to dry for several days.

'Washing' here means 'collection of clothes that have been washed'. 'Washings' could only mean 'several washing processes', and this plural form is much less common than the singular.

It will be obvious that the noun 'washing' is formed by adding '-ing' to the verb 'wash'. Very many nouns (or 'verb-nouns') can be formed in the same way, but there are no firm rules as to whether they can or cannot be used in the plural. A list of words in common use is given on page 227.

Collective Nouns: Misuse of Plural

A COLLECTIVE noun or GROUP noun is one which in the singular refers to a *set of objects*. It can have both singular and plural forms; but the plural means several *sets of objects*, not several objects. Confusion here often causes the plural to be misused, for example:

28 Army

Wrong: The king sent his armies to besiege the city.

Correct: The king sent his army *or* soldiers *or* troops to besiege the city.

Normally a king would have only one army under his command. The plural in *-ies* would be used if the army of one power were facing the army of another power.

29 Beard

Wrong: He shaved off his beards.
Correct: He shaved off his beard.

One person can have only one beard. 'Beards' implies different people, each with a beard:

> They were told to shave off their beards.

30 Enemy

Wrong: He learned that the town had fallen to the enemies.
Correct: He learned that the town had fallen to the enemy.

When 'enemy' means 'hostile armed forces', it should be used in the singular only.

31 Executive

Wrong: The executives were compelled to resign, and new elections were held.
Correct: The members of the executive were compelled to resign, and new elections were held.

'The executive' here means 'the executive authority' or 'the Executive Council', and is used in a mainly *political* context where there may be a distinction between executive and legislative bodies. The persons who are members of it cannot be called individually 'an executive', or in the plural 'the executives'. When 'executives' does refer to an individual person, the context must be that of business or administration:

> He has become one of the top executives in a major oil company.

32 Fleet

Wrong: In December 1941 Japan attacked the American fleets at Pearl Harbour.
Correct: In December 1941 Japan attacked the American fleet *or* ships at Pearl Harbour.

'Fleet' behaves very much like 'army' (number 28).

33 Grass

Wrong: Nduka told the Principal that all the grasses had been cut.

Correct: Nduka told the Principal that all the grass had been cut.

'Grasses' would only be used in a discussion among people interested in botany, who might want to distinguish between different types of grass.

34 Hair

Wrong: Though young, he had lost most of his hairs.

Correct: Though young, he had lost most of his hair.

Here the hair is considered as one mass; there is no point in thinking of all the thousands of individual hairs one by one. But this sentence is correct:

> She plucked a few hairs from her eye-brows.

35 Issue, offspring

Wrong: They have been married for three years but have no issues *or* offsprings.

Correct: They have been married for three years but have no issue *or* offspring *or* children.

'Offspring' is uncountable. 'Issue' meaning 'children' has no plural form; but 'issue' meaning 'topic for debate' has both singular and plural forms:

> Several important issues were raised at the meeting.

36 People

Wrong: Many peoples are compelled to live in one tiny area of the city.

Correct: Many people are compelled to live in one tiny area of the city.

Wrong: Peoples never thank you for telling them the truth about themselves.

Correct: People never thank you for telling them the truth about themselves.

'People' only has the plural -*s* when it means 'race':

> The peoples of the world may have a common origin.

37 Vocabulary
Wrong: Philip speaks English correctly but lacks vocabularies.

Correct: Philip speaks English correctly but lacks vocabulary.

'Vocabulary' means a collection – often a list – of words and their meanings. It can be used occasionally in the plural when referring to more than one language, for example:

> The vocabularies of the Bantu languages resemble one another closely.

Singular and Plural Forms Confused

In some of the examples in the previous section the plural form of a word has a different meaning from the singular, and the two may get confused. Here are some more examples:

38 Character
Wrong: Gloria was almost friendless as a result of her bad characters.

Correct: Gloria was almost friendless as a result of her bad character.

One person has only one character. But when 'character' means 'person' or 'individual', it can be used both in the singular and the plural, as in the following sentences:

> Okoh is a peculiar character – he never visits his neighbours.
> There are many striking characters in Shakespeare's plays.

39 Content and contents

Wrong: Mrs Omole emptied the content of the bag over the table.

Correct: Mrs Omole emptied the contents of the bag over the table.

'Contents', plural, is used for the things found in any container, such as a bag, a jar, a house, or even a book. (There is a list of contents at the front of this book.) 'Content', singular, is another word for 'amount' or 'proportion' which can be measured, for example:

> This beer has a low alcohol content.

40 Damage

Wrong: The storm caused many damages to houses in our town.

Correct: The storm caused a lot of damage *or* much damage to houses in our town.

'Damage' meaning 'injury', 'destruction', is uncountable. The plural can only be used in a legal context, where it means an amount of money claimed or paid in compensation for injury:

> The judge awarded him a large sum of money as damages.

41 Fund

Wrong: This is the time of the year when we always lack fund.

Correct: This is the time of the year when we always lack funds.

When 'fund' means money in general (from whatever sources) it must be used in the plural with -s. When it means money specially raised for a certain purpose, it can be used both in the singular and in the plural:

> A fund has been launched by the Governor to help the disabled.

42 Gossip

Wrong: The gossips I have heard concerning you do not please me.

Correct: The gossip I have heard concerning you does not please me.

The rumours I have heard concerning you do not please me.

'Gossip' can be used in three different ways:
1 as a noun with no plural form meaning 'idle talk', 'rumour' (as in the example);
2 as a verb meaning 'talk idly or irresponsibly', in which case it may take -s;
3 as a noun with both singular and plural forms meaning 'someone who gossips', for example:

The old women in my village are a lot of gossips.

43 Property

Wrong: The thieves stole all my properties.
Correct: The thieves stole all my property.

'Property' meaning 'personal possessions' is an uncountable noun. It is countable (1) when it means 'house' as used by estate agents and others involved in the buying and selling of houses; (2) when it means 'characteristic', 'peculiarity', for example:

Reaction with acids to form oxides is a property of metals. What are the properties of hydrogen?

44 Quarters

Wrong: He is occupying a fine quarters *or* a fine quarter in the New Lay-Out.

Correct: He is occupying some fine quarters *or* a fine house in the New Lay-Out.

'Quarters' meaning 'house' is plural, has no singular form, and cannot be used with 'a'. 'Quarter' meaning 'area of a town' can be used both in the singular and the plural, for example:

He lives in an attractive quarter of the town.
He toured the poorer quarters of the city.

45 Wire

Wrong: Barbed wires were used for the fencing of the compound.

Correct: Barbed wire was used for the fencing of the compound.

A wire is a thin strip of metal, and as such is countable; but a collection or mass of wires is 'wire', an uncountable noun. In the above example there is no point in thinking of the individual, countable wires.

The plural could be used like this:

Join these two wires together, or you will not get any current.

Unusual Singulars and Plurals

In addition to the well-known nouns with irregular plurals mentioned on page 1 there are certain nouns with unusual singular or plural forms that cause problems:

46 Cattle

Wrong: A lot of cattles have died during the drought.
Correct: A lot of cattle have died during the drought.

'Cattle' is a collective noun and plural in form, though it can never take -*s*.

47 News

Wrong: The news you have given me are very surprising.

Correct: The news you have given me is very surprising.

Wrong: I received a sad news yesterday.
Correct: I received a sad piece of news yesterday.

'News' looks like a plural noun because of its -*s*, but it behaves as a singular.

48 Pyjamas

Wrong: She put his pyjama on his bed.
Correct: She put his pyjamas on his bed.

When it means the set – or sets – of one shirt and one pair of trousers used for sleeping, this word is used in the plural. The singular, 'pyjama', is used adjectivally to distinguish the shirt or trousers from other types of shirts and trousers, thus:

> She hung his pyjama shirt out to dry.

49 Series

Wrong: The Matron gave the nurse series of warnings.
Correct: The Matron gave the nurse a series of warnings.

Although it looks like a plural because of the -*s*, 'series' can also be used in the singular, and is more often found in that form.

50 Species

Wrong: That bird must be a specie of hawk.
Correct: That bird must be a species of hawk.

'Species' can be either singular or plural in meaning, and when the meaning is plural it must behave as a plural apart from not changing its form. For example:

> There are many species of carnivores in Africa.

There is a singular form 'specie', but it has a very specialized use in finance, meaning 'coins, not paper money'.

51 Trousers

Wrong: Kola went to the market to buy a new trouser.
Correct: Kola went to the market to buy a new pair of trousers *or* some new trousers.

'Trousers' is a plural word with no singular form. 'Some new trousers' can mean one pair, or more than one pair.

52 Whereabouts

Wrong: His whereabout was unknown to me.
Correct: His whereabouts was *or* His whereabouts were
unknown to me.

'Whereabouts' meaning 'location' is found only in the plural, but it can be followed by either a singular or a plural verb.

Special Forms used in Idioms

In certain well-known idioms a noun may have a fixed singular or plural form. Errors occur when this is varied, for example:

53 At all costs

Wrong: You must go to see your mother at all cost.
Correct: You must go to see your mother at all costs.

'At all costs' (with -*s*) is an idiom meaning 'no matter what the cost may be to you'. Very similar in meaning is 'at any cost', but here 'cost' has no -*s*.

54 In fear of, in hope of

Wrong: They lived in fears of being arrested.
Correct: They lived in fear of being arrested.

'Fear' is used in the singular in fixed phrases like 'in fear of', 'for fear of',no matter how many people have the fear. In other contexts the plural can be used, for example:

> Their fears of rejection were realized.
> I have many fears concerning the future.

'Hope' behaves like 'fear'.

55 Have the guts

Wrong: He didn't have the gut to tell the President the truth.
Correct: He didn't have the guts to tell the President the truth.

The 'gut' or 'guts' means the entrails of an animal. The

plural form used in this idiom means 'courage'. This idiom is not to be used in writing or in formal speech.

56 Pull someone's leg

Wrong: You're pulling my legs. I know Nkechi is married already.

Correct: You're pulling my leg. I know Nkechi is married already.

There is only one leg in this idiom meaning 'to tell a lie as a joke', or 'tease'. If more than one person is being teased, the idiom is best avoided, like this:

> You're teasing us. We know Nkechi is married already.

To say either 'You're pulling our leg' or 'You're pulling our legs' would sound strange.

57 Run for dear life

Wrong: The monster was not far behind them, and they were running for their dear lives.

Correct: The monster was not far behind them, and they were running for dear life.

In this idiom, which means 'run as fast as possible', 'life' should never be made plural, and no possessive ('his', 'her', 'their', etc.) may be used. The idiom is in any case a cliché, and should be avoided. (See Chapter 15.)

58 At loggerheads

Wrong: Mr Bosede was at loggerhead with all his colleagues.

Correct: Mr Bosede was at loggerheads with all his colleagues.

In the idiom 'be at loggerheads with', meaning 'be in conflict with', the plural must always be used.

59 Throw one's weight about

Wrong: Senior to us he may be, but I hate people who throw their weights about.

Correct: Senior to us he may be, but I hate people who throw their weight about.

The plural, 'weights', must not be used in this idiom.

Now that you have looked at these errors concerning the formation of nouns, turn to the back of the book and do Exercises 1–7.

2 Adjectives

Adjectives describe or give more details about nouns: e.g., *men* (noun); *old men* (*old* – adjective). The position of an adjective is usually either (i) before a noun (e.g. *the new school*) or (ii) after a 'linking verb' (see page 207), such as *is*: e.g. *The grass is green.* Occasionally adjectives can be used after a noun, and they are used after certain pronouns: *the person responsible*, *something good*, *all those present*.

In the examples above one-word adjectives have been used. There are other words which can function as one-word adjectives, notably

(a) *Participles*. (See page 210.) For example: *disturbing* news; a *broken* window; The children are *excited*.

(b) *Nouns*. as in: a *shoe* factory; a *Biology* assignment; a *customs* officer.

In addition to the adjectives listed in the dictionary, there is a huge number of ADJECTIVALS, or adjectives consisting of more than one word. (See page 197.)

Errors in Adjective Formation

Many adjectives are formed by adding a suffix or ending to nouns or verbs, such as *-ous*, *-ful*, *-less*, *-ic*, *-al*, *-ive*, and so on. Very many are formed by adding *-ing* or *-ed* to a verb. This is the present or past participle of the verb used as an adjective. (See pages 54 and 210.) Some errors arise through choice of the wrong suffix, or through failure to add a suffix.

60 Insulting
Wrong: He is always making insultive remarks.
Correct: He is always making insulting remarks.

61 Cowardly

Wrong: He is a coward man.
Correct: He is a coward *or* a cowardly man *or* cowardly.

'Coward' is a noun, 'cowardly' the adjective derived from it.

62 Advanced

Wrong: He studies at an Advance Teachers' College.
Correct: He studies at an Advanced Teachers' College.

63 Surprised

Wrong: I am surprise to hear she passed with distinction.
Correct: I am surprised to hear she passed with distinction.

64 Mature, matured

Wrong: He is a matured politician.
Correct: He is a mature politician.

Mature, with no *-d*, is the usual form of the adjective used before a noun and meaning 'adult', 'experienced'. *Matured* usually functions as the past simple or past participle of the verb *mature*, which means 'become mature', 'become ripe', 'come to fruition':

My insurance policy has matured.

65 Welcome, welcomed

Wrong: So you are back at last! You are welcomed.
Correct: So you are back at last! You are welcome.

In saying the very words 'You are welcome' the speaker expresses a welcome, and in this context 'welcome' is an adjective which does not change its form. But in other contexts it can be used as a verb and can take *-d*:

He was warmly welcomed on his return from abroad. (People received him happily, they perhaps hugged and kissed him, or sang songs in his honour.)

Errors in use of Adjectives as Nouns

Some adjectives can function as nouns; that is, preceded by an article and with no noun following. They must nevertheless be used with great caution.

66 The poor
Wrong: The poors often do not benefit from education.
Correct: The poor often do not benefit from education.

67 The blind
Wrong: She wanted to establish a special hospital for the blinds.
Correct: She wanted to establish a special hospital for the blind.

Other adjectives in the same group as *the poor* and *the blind* are: *the deaf, the rich, the old, the young, the hungry, the homeless, the unemployed, the bereaved, the wise.* Rules for their use are: they have plural meaning; they can be preceded by 'the' but not by 'a' or 'an'; they cannot take *-s*.

68 Foolish
Wrong: Who told you to do that? You are a foolish.
Correct: Who told you to do that? You are a fool *or* foolish *or* a foolish person.

The adjective cannot be used by itself as a noun.

69 Final
Wrong: Whatever the Chief says is the final.
Correct: Whatever the Chief says is final.

We can say 'the last', 'the best', 'the first', and so on, but not 'the final'.

70 The British, the French, etc. (Nationality Adjectives.)
Wrong: He is a British. He is a French. She is a Spanish.
Correct: He is British. He is French. She is Spanish.

In these examples, an adjective ('British', 'French', 'Spanish') cannot be used as a singular noun. It can however be used as a plural noun, just like 'the poor', etc.:

> The French spend a lot of money on food.
> The British spend less on food than the French.

Likewise it is possible to say 'the English' but not 'an English', 'the Irish', but not 'an Irish', 'the Dutch', but not 'a Dutch'.

There are some nationality adjectives which cannot serve as nouns at all, such as 'Polish', 'Finnish', 'Swedish'.

The majority of nationality adjectives, and also adjectives indicating ethnicity, can function as nouns, and can have both singular and plural forms:

> He is a Nigerian *or* Nigerian. The Nigerians.
> She is a Ghanian *or* Ghanaian. The Ghanaians.
> He is a Kikuyu *or* Kikuyu. The Kikuyus.
> You are an Arab *or* Arab. The Arabs.

71 Hausa, Swahili, etc. (Language Adjectives.)

Wrong: He spoke to me in Hausa language.
Correct: He spoke to me in Hausa.

Wrong: She greeted me in Swahili language.
Correct: She greeted me in Swahili.

There is no need to add the word 'language' here, where it is clear that the Hausa language or the Swahili language is meant. In other contexts a noun must be added:

> I am writing a book on Hausa literature.

Errors in the Adjectival use of Nouns

Some nouns can be used adjectivally both (i) before a noun and (ii) after the same noun in an *of* (or *in* etc.) phrase, as for example in: *an economics student, a student of economics; the Chemistry Department, the Department of Chemistry; a newspaper*

editor, the editor of a newspaper; his Enugu trip, his trip to Enugu.
Some nouns cannot be used in both positions, however; some can only be used before, some can only be used after other nouns. Some can be used in both positions, with different meanings in each. Finally, nouns which stand for human beings or which are personal names can be used in both positions, and when used before another noun have an added *-'s: the office of the Manager, the Manager's office; the appointment of Mr Isa, Mr Isa's appointment.* This often indicates possession, and is known as 'possessive', or 'genitive' *-'s.*

72 Of + noun wrongly used

Wrong: He works for a company of oil.
Correct: He works for an oil company.

Wrong: This mechanic can do balancing of wheels.
Correct: This mechanic can do wheel-balancing.

Wrong: I must go to the bank to ask for a new book of cheques.
Correct: I must go to the bank to ask for a new cheque book.

Wrong: She saved up her money to buy a machine of sewing.
Correct: She saved up her money to buy a sewing machine.

73 Nouns wrongly used before other nouns

Wrong: The museum houses many art-works.
Correct: The museum houses many works of art.

Wrong: I am thirsty. Please make me a teacup.
Correct: I am thirsty. Please make me a cup of tea.

'A teacup' means 'a cup which is used for drinking tea'; 'a cup of tea' means 'some tea, to be drunk out of a cup'.

The correct placement of nouns used adjectivally has to be learned for each noun. Note also that when one noun precedes another, sometimes a hyphen is used to make them into a new 'compound' noun, sometimes not. Once again the rule for each combination of nouns has to be learned individually.

74 Wrong use of the possessive -'s
Wrong: A huge statue stood in the room's corner.
Correct: A huge statue stood in the corner of the room.

Wrong: The triangle's base measured 10 centimetres.
Correct: The base of the triangle measured 10 centimetres.

Wrong: I cannot undo my shirt's top button.
Correct: I cannot undo the top button of my shirt.

Wrong: Please remove this apple's skin for me.
Correct: Please remove the skin of this apple for me.

75 Wrong use of plural -s in compound adjectives
Wrong: He went for a five-miles walk.
Correct: He went for a five-mile walk.

In this example the distance covered by the walk is five miles. But when this numeral + noun phrase is used as an adjectival before another noun, the *-s* must be dropped. Likewise say *a four-inch nail; a three-year-old girl; a ten-volume encyclopaedia*, etc.

Errors in the use of Comparatives and Superlatives

Those using this book should already be able to form the comparative and superlative of any adjective correctly. (For example, adjective: *poor*; comparative: *poorer*; superlative: *poorest*.) Some problems are caused by the existence of a few irregular forms, such as *good – better – best* and *bad – worse – worst*, or by the misuse of the comparative and superlative forms, as follows:

76 Better
Wrong: You see these two carvings? This one is more better than that one.

Correct: You see these two carvings? This one is better
than that one.

'Better' is by itself the comparative of 'good', so 'more'
here is redundant.

77 Superior
Wrong: He said that a Volvo was more superior to a
Mercedes.

Correct: He said that a Volvo was superior to a
Mercedes.

Once again, 'superior' is already a comparative adjective,
so 'more' is not needed.

78 Wrong omission of comparative before **than**
Wrong: This exhibition is exciting in every way than
the previous one.

Correct: This exhibition is more exciting in every way
than the previous one.

Wrong: This year's festival was very successful than
last year's.

Correct: This year's festival was more *or* much more
successful than last year's.

79 Wrong use of **the worst**
Wrong: It hardly rained last year, but this year's
drought is the worst.

Correct: It hardly rained last year, but this year's
drought is worse.

'The worst' is a superlative form of 'bad', and must
describe something which is compared with more than
one other thing. It could be used correctly like this:

It hardly rained last year, but this year's drought
is the worst within living memory.

80 Wrong use of **less**
Wrong: He said the value put on the house was too
less.

Correct: He said the value put on the house was too small.

You can never say 'too less'. 'Less' is a comparative adjective and is usually followed by 'than':

> The value he put on the house was less than I expected.

Now turn to the back of the book and do Exercises 8 and 9.

3 Articles

Articles are among a small group of highly important and useful words which are known as DETERMINERS. Other determiners are dealt with in the next chapter; this chapter features articles only.

There are just two articles in English, the DEFINITE ARTICLE ('the') and the INDEFINITE ARTICLE ('a', or 'an' before a following word that begins with a vowel). They are used before nouns. The problem lies in deciding when to use them and when not to use them, and this leads to many common errors, such as those which are set out below. Some guidelines are given on pages 199–202, and these should be studied along with this chapter.

'A' or 'an' wrongly used

One general rule to follow is that uncountable nouns, as well as not having any plural in -s, must not be preceded by 'a' or 'an'. Hence you are advised to look once again at numbers 2 to 27 and remember not to use 'a' or 'an' with any of the words listed there. Mistakes like the following will then be avoided:

81 Advice

Wrong: Let me give you an advice, which you may not like to hear.

Correct: Let me give you some advice *or* a piece of advice, which you may not like to hear.

But at this point note also that some nouns can be either countable or uncountable, depending on the meaning. 'Advice', for example, is uncountable when it means 'counsel' as in the example above, but countable when it means 'formal notification' in a business context, for example:

> The Manager received an advice from the Ikeja branch.

Likewise 'accommodation' is uncountable when it means 'lodgings', but countable when it means 'settlement', 'compromise', in which case it can be preceded by 'an'.

Errors with other nouns

82 Attention

Wrong: Uchendu needs a medical attention.
Correct: Uchendu needs medical attention.

Wrong: Please pay an attention to what I am saying.
Correct: Please pay attention to what I am saying.

83 Concern

Wrong: The news of the fighting causes us a concern.
Correct: The news of the fighting causes us concern.

'Concern' cannot be preceded by 'a' when it means 'anxiety'. It may be preceded by 'a' when it means 'business venture':

> His timber company has at last become a going concern.

84 Credit

Wrong: A credit should be given to him for his outspokenness before the Committee.
Correct: Credit should be given to him for his outspokenness before the Committee.

Wrong: He was given a credit for the successful attack on the bridge.
Correct: He was given credit for the successful attack on the bridge.

In these examples 'credit' means something like 'due praise', and is uncountable. It is countable when it means

(i) 'source of honour'; (ii) 'grade obtained in academic work':

> A great writer is a credit to his country.
> It was a great credit to him that he was able to bring up his brother's children as well as his own.
> I got a credit in General Science.

85 Harm

Wrong: Your arrogance will do a great harm to your cause.

Correct: Your arrogance will do great harm to your cause.

86 Hearsay

Wrong: Everyone is talking about their impending divorce, but to me it is all a hearsay.

Correct: Everyone is talking about their impending divorce, but to me it is all hearsay.

87 Help

Wrong: Being in difficulties, Paul came to me to ask for a help.

Correct: Being in difficulties, Paul came to me to ask for help.

Wrong: They are both old and infirm, and need a help.

Correct: They are both old and infirm, and need help.

'Help' is preceded by 'a' when it follows some part of the verb 'be':

> I was a great help to him when he was out of work.

88 Lunch (and other meals).

Wrong: You must come and have a lunch with me some time.

Correct: You must come and have lunch with me some time.

Wrong: She was invited to have a dinner with the Governor's wife.

Correct: She was invited to have dinner with the Governor's wife.

'Lunch' ('dinner', etc.) must not be preceded by 'a' in the phrase 'have lunch' ('dinner', etc.). At other times 'a' may be used if a *specific* meal is in question, or if a choice is implied:

> A dinner at that restaurant is very expensive.

The meaning is that the price of the dinner there may vary, but always there will be a large bill to pay. The word 'meal' itself is countable.

89 Permission

Wrong: I did not give Yohana a permission to travel home.

Correct: I did not give Yohana permission to travel home.

The related word 'permit', meaning 'written permission' or 'licence', is preceded by 'a':

> I applied to the Customs Department for a permit.

90 Treatment

Wrong: He had a skin complaint, and went to hospital for a treatment.

Correct: He had a skin complaint, and went to hospital for treatment.

91 Weather

Wrong: Have you ever known a weather like this in June?

Correct: Have you ever known weather like this in June?

92 Work

Wrong: He returned to university to do a research work.

Correct: He returned to university to do research work.

Wrong: He can't find a work, and depends on his brother.

Correct: He can't find work, *or* any work, *or* a job, and depends on his brother.

'Work' is not preceded by 'a' when it means 'effort' or 'paid employment'. It is preceded by 'a' when it means 'something achieved':

This new play is a work of genius.

'A' or 'an' wrongly omitted

The converse of the rule that uncountable nouns must not be preceded by 'a' or 'an' is that countable nouns must be preceded by 'a' or 'an'. Errors occur when it is omitted:

93 An accident
Wrong: If you drive at that speed, you will have accident.

Correct: If you drive at that speed, you will have an accident.

94 A bath
Wrong: He went to take bath *or* to have bath.

Correct: He went to take a bath *or* to have a bath.

95 A chance
Wrong: I didn't have *or* I didn't get chance to see her last week.

Correct: I didn't have *or* I didn't get a chance to see her last week.

Also see number 251.

96 A contract
Wrong: He got contract from the Ministry.

Correct: He got a contract from the Ministry.

97 A headache
Wrong: She had headache, and took some tablets.

Correct: She had a headache, and took some tablets.

With 'toothache' and 'stomach-ache', 'a' may be either used or left out. For other illnesses, see page 220.

98 A lie
Wrong: I will not tell you lie: he has been sacked.
Correct: I will not tell you a lie: he has been sacked.

99 A mistake
Wrong: Try not to make mistake in the calculation.
Correct: Try not to make a mistake in the calculation.

100 A name
Wrong: You will not make name for yourself merely by boasting.
Correct: You will not make a name for yourself merely by boasting.

'Make a name' means 'earn a good reputation'.

101 A price
Wrong: I said the jacket was too expensive, and asked him to give me better price.
Correct: I said the jacket was too expensive, and asked him to give me a better price.

Also see number 574.

102 A role
Wrong: He played prominent role in the liberation of his country.
Correct: He played a prominent role in the liberation of his country.

103 A solution
Wrong: We must find solution to this problem.
Correct: We must find a solution to this problem.

In this example, 'the' could be used instead of 'a'; this would mean that only one solution is expected.

104 A surprise, a shock (and other emotions)

Wrong: It gave me great surprise *or* great shock to hear of your resignation.

Correct: It gave me a great surprise *or* a great shock to hear of your resignation.

'A' must always be used before 'surprise' and 'shock' when they are nouns; they are countable. Other words expressing emotion tend to be uncountable:

It gives me great pleasure to be with you today.

But after the verb 'be' such nouns become countable, and 'a' or 'an' may be used:

It was a great pleasure to hear of your son's appointment.

'The' wrongly used

Errors frequently occur where the definite article is concerned, because most, if not all nouns must sometimes be preceded by the definite article and at other times must not be. It is for this reason that certain words appearing in this section appear again later. (See numbers 105–113 and then numbers 116–124.)

When making the choice between using and not using the definite article, it is necessary to grasp the fact that a given noun can refer either to *one* specific or particular object, or to *all* objects in the set which the noun refers to. In the first case we talk of SPECIFIC reference, in the second of GENERIC reference.

Rules for the use of the definite article are given in the chapter 'Notes on Grammar' on pages 199–202. Note here that it is often with uncountable nouns, once again, that problems arise. The definite article is used with uncountable nouns having *specific* reference; it *is not* used before uncountable nouns having *generic* reference.

105 Love

Wrong: The love is a virtue few people really practise.

Correct: Love is a virtue few people really practise.

106 Transport

Wrong: We are neglecting the railways, and spending too much on the road transport.

Correct: We are neglecting the railways, and spending too much on road transport.

107 Society

Wrong: The society disapproves of those who do not respect its traditions.

Correct: Society disapproves of those who do not respect its traditions.

'The' can however be used with 'Society' when it has a capital 'S' and means a professional body or a club, etc.:

> The society will be obliged to you for your annual subscription.

108 Defence

Wrong: The superpowers spend colossal sums of money on the defence.

Correct: The superpowers spend colossal sums of money on defence.

109 Administration

Wrong: I loathe the administration; I prefer teaching.

Correct: I loathe administration; I prefer teaching.

110 Light

Wrong: The light travels at a speed of 180,000 miles per second.

Correct: Light travels at a speed of 180,000 miles per second.

111 Singing

Wrong: The singing is a skill one should cultivate.

Correct: Singing is a skill one should cultivate.

112 School

Wrong: The whole world now accepts that children should go to the school.

Correct: The whole world now accepts that children should go to school.

113 Church
Wrong: When Emeka left his home town, he stopped going to the church.
Correct: When Emeka left his home town, he stopped going to church.

'Church' has a capital letter and is preceded by the definite article when it refers to an institution:

> He was examining the doctrines of the Church.

The definite article is not however used before 'Church' if 'Church' is used as an adjective before another noun having generic reference:

> She is very much interested in Church affairs.

114 University
Wrong: He wants to go to the university after he leaves school.
Correct: He wants to go to university after he leaves school.

If there were only one university in the country in question, university would be written with a capital 'U', and 'He wants to go to the University' would be correct.

115 Geography
Wrong: We are now studying the West African geography.
Correct: We are now studying West African geography.

'The' wrongly omitted

See the general remarks at the beginning of the previous section.

116 Love
Wrong: Love he had for her was excessive.
Correct: The love he had for her was excessive.

117 Transport

Wrong: We need more roads and railways to facilitate transport of goods over long distances.

Correct: We need more roads and railways to facilitate the transport of goods over long distances.

118 Society

Wrong: Society of Ancient Greece was based on slavery.

Correct: The society of Ancient Greece was based on slavery.

119 Defence

Wrong: We must give priority to defence of our borders.

Correct: We must give priority to the defence of our borders.

120 Administration

Wrong: Improvements in administration of the University are needed.

Correct: Improvements in the administration of the University are needed.

Note that when 'administration' refers to the particular set of people charged with administrative responsibility, it always has specific reference, it is written with a capital 'A', and has the definite article before it:

> The students wanted to become part of the Administration.

'Government' behaves in much the same way.

121 Light

Wrong: Light of the sun gives light to the moon.
Correct: The light of the sun gives light to the moon.

122 Singing

Wrong: She stopped to listen to singing of the birds.
Correct: She stopped to listen to the singing of the birds.

123 School

Wrong: The teacher went back to school to referee a
match.

Correct: The teacher went back to the school to referee
a match.

Sometimes there is only a slight difference of meaning
between 'school' and 'the school', and in the context of
just one sentence either would be correct:

Ola is not in school this morning. (He is at
home.)
Ola is not in the school this morning. (He has
gone somewhere.)

124 Church

Wrong: He entered church, and sat down at the back.

Correct: He entered the church, and sat down at the
back.

'The' with proper nouns

Proper nouns are names of specific people and things. They are
distinguished chiefly by being written with capital letters. All
nouns that are not proper nouns are called common nouns.
Some proper nouns require the definite article; some do not.
Here are some guidelines:

1 *No definite article required*: Names of persons, days, months,
  and festivals; religions; certain geographical features (towns
  and other place names, most countries, continents, lakes,
  islands, mountains, hills, states and provinces); prominent
  features of towns (streets, buildings, bridges, parks, etc.);
  most planets and stars; magazines.

2 *Definite article required*: Titles (where the personal name is not
  also given); a few countries and political organizations;
  oceans, rivers, deserts, hill and mountain ranges; newspapers; hotels.

3 *Educational institutions*: The name of an educational institution usually has two parts: a noun such as 'school',

'university', etc., and a description such as 'Government Secondary'. If this description comes *after* the noun, 'the' must be used; if the description comes *before* the noun, 'the' is normally not used.

Common errors in this area include the following:

125 Country
Wrong: Nairobi is the capital of the Kenya.
Correct: Nairobi is the capital of Kenya.

126 State
Wrong: Cocoa is grown in many parts of the Oyo State.
Correct: Cocoa is grown in many parts of Oyo State.

127 Continent
Wrong: He spent several years in the North America.
Correct: He spent several years in North America.

128 Mountain
Wrong: His birthplace lies not far from the Mount Kilimanjaro.
Correct: His birthplace lies not far from Mount Kilimanjaro.

129 Religion
Wrong: The Islam originated in Arabia.
Correct: Islam originated in Arabia.

130 Festival
Wrong: On the Christmas Day the birth of Christ is celebrated.
Correct: On Christmas Day the birth of Christ is celebrated.

131 Building
Wrong: They were married at the Christchurch Cathedral.
Correct: They were married at Christchurch Cathedral.

132 Airport
Wrong: Our plane will soon land at the Lilongwe Airport.

Correct: Our plane will soon land at Lilongwe Airport.

133 Street
Wrong: Let us go for a stroll along the Independence Way.

Correct: Let us go for a stroll along Independence Way.

134 Ocean
Wrong: He sailed across Indian Ocean.

Correct: He sailed across the Indian Ocean.

135 River
Wrong: They built a bridge over River Niger.

Correct: They built a bridge over the River Niger.

136 Country
Wrong: He went for further studies in USSR.

Correct: He went for further studies in the USSR.

Likewise 'the USA' (or, in full, 'the United States of America'), 'the UK' ('the United Kingdom'), 'the UNO' ('the United Nations Organization'), 'the OAU' ('the Organization of African Unity').

137 Empire
Wrong: They were busy studying the history of Ghana Empire.

Correct: They were busy studying the history of the Ghana Empire. (*Or*: the Empire of Ghana.)

138 Desert
Wrong: There are many oases in Sahara Desert.

Correct: There are many oases in the Sahara Desert.

139 College
Wrong: He is the Principal of the Government College, Katsina.

Correct: He is the Principal of Government College, Katsina.

140 University

Wrong: She lectures at University of Dakar.
Correct: 1 She lectures at the University of Dakar.
2 She lectures at Dakar University.

One final word in this section. Wrong use of the articles in English will rarely cause you to be misunderstood, so that errors like those listed above may not be considered very serious. At the same time, proper use of the articles may be regarded as one of the hallmarks of the really careful speaker or writer wishing to bring his performance in English up to a high standard.

You are now advised to do Exercises 10 to 13.

4 Other Determiners

Apart from Articles, the class of Determiners includes Amount Words or Quantifiers (*some, any, much, many, more, most, several, no, few, a few, little, a little, enough, all, each, every, both, either, neither*); Demonstratives (*this, that, these, those*); Possessives (*my, your, his, her, its, our, their*); Numerals (*one, two, three*, etc.; *first, second, third*, etc.; *half, one-third*, etc.); and a few others. Determiners are used before nouns, like adjectives, and sometimes more than one can be used. They can also function as pronouns.

Errors include the use of the wrong determiner; the wrong ordering of determiners when more than one can be used; and the redundant or unnecessary use of a determiner. For guidance about the order of determiners, see pages 202–4.

Errors in the use of determiners can be very serious indeed. Use of the wrong determiner, for example, can change the whole meaning of a sentence.

Use of the wrong Determiner

141 **Most** wrongly used

Example 1 100 people were in a building when a fire broke out; 40 of the people died.

Wrong: Most of the people died.
Correct: Many of the people died.

'Most' would only be correct if more than 50 died, and is best used if 80 or 90 died.

Example 2 There was an outbreak of meningitis in our town, and 5 cases were reported in a school of 200 pupils.

>*Wrong:*   Most of the pupils caught the disease.
>*Correct:*   A few of the pupils caught the disease.

142 **Another** and **more** confused
>*Wrong:*   You will have to bring another money to
>   complete the payment.
>*Correct:*   You will have to bring (some) more money to
>   complete the payment.

'Money' is an uncountable noun, and cannot be preceded by 'another'. 'Another' is used with countable nouns, for example:

>Find me another biro; this one is used up.

143 **Few, a few** confused
>*Wrong:*   We invited all our friends, but a few of them
>   turned up.
>*Correct:*   We invited all our friends, but few turned up.

The use of 'but' shows that there is a contrast between the number of friends invited and the small number who turned up. When you want to stress the smallness of the number in this way, use 'few', not 'a few'. It is possible also to say, however, 'only a few'.

144 **Little, a little** confused
>*Wrong:*   A: Do you take milk? B: Yes, you can put little
>   in my cup.
>*Correct:*   A: Do you take milk? B: Yes, you can put a
>   little in my cup.

(In examples like this, 'A' and 'B' indicate two different speakers.) This error is like the previous one in reverse. 'Yes, you can put little . . .' does not make sense, because there is no need for emphasis on the smallness of the amount. But this is a correct sentence:

>She gave him a strong cup of tea, saying that
>there was little milk left.

145 **Whole** wrongly used

Wrong: The whole certificates were missing.
Correct: All the certificates *or* All of the certificates were missing.

Wrong: The whole streets were flooded.
Correct: All the streets were flooded.

'The whole' may not be used with the plural of nouns, but only with the singular.

> The whole street was flooded.

This sentence means that all parts of the street were flooded. There are several other ways of saying this last sentence:

> The entire street *or* All the street *or* The whole of the street *or* All of the street was flooded.

We can say 'the whole of the' as well as 'the whole'; 'all of the' as well as 'all', though we cannot say 'the entire of the'.

'*A whole*' is used to emphasize the idea of completeness, when it is possible to think of a part as well as the whole:

> He ate a whole loaf of bread.
> A whole platoon was wiped out.

146 **Some** and **any** confused

Wrong: A loving father would not like to beat some of his children.
Correct: A loving father would not like to beat any of his children.

The sentence means that a loving father would like to beat none of his children. When 'none' is the intended meaning, say 'not . . . any' instead of 'not . . . some'.

147 Wrong use of **any** after **-ever** words

Wrong: Whenever Uju enters any market, she buys something.

Correct: Whenever Uju enters a market, she buys something.

It is not necessary to say 'any' instead of 'a' here, because the use of 'whenever' by itself ensures that 'market' is any market and not a particular market.

148 **Both** and **either** confused

Wrong: There is no sound coming out of both speakers.
Correct: There is no sound coming out of either speaker.

'Either' is required because of the preceding 'no'.

149 Wrong use of **the** instead of a possessive

Wrong: He had a boil on the neck.
Correct: He had a boil on his neck.

'The' is used instead of a possessive adjective when reference is made to human beings in general:

> The most complex organ of a man's body is the brain *or* his brain.

It may be used also for particular persons when the person is referred to earlier in the sentence:

> When they opened him up, they found his stomach in a bad condition; the kidneys *or* his kidneys were also affected.

Here, 'the kidneys' is possible because it comes after 'his stomach'.

150 **His** and **her** confused

John and Mary are brother and sister.

Wrong: Mary introduced me to John and said that he was his brother.
Correct: Mary introduced me to John and said that he was her brother.

Here only 'her brother' is correct, because we are speaking of the brother of Mary. Possessives must refer to the possessor, not to the thing or person possessed.

If the situation were different – if John were not the brother of Mary – then 'his brother' could be correct, and would mean that John was the brother of some other person, boy or man, not mentioned in the sentence.

This is a very common error, and one easy to make if your first language does not have separate masculine and feminine pronouns and possessives, or if in your first language possessives refer to the thing or person possessed.

151 Wrong use of **her**

Wrong: The Association needs the co-operation of all her members.
Correct: The Association needs the co-operation of all its members.

Wrong: The Government in her wisdom has decided to change the law.
Correct: The Government in its wisdom has decided to change the law.

The possessive 'her' normally indicates a female possessor. Occasionally it can refer to one of certain permanent or august institutions that command affection: one's native land, university, church, etc. 'Government' is not regarded as feminine.

152 Wrong use of demonstratives

Wrong: 'Good evening, ladies and gentlemen. In those days, a man did not use a foreign tongue to speak to his own people'.
Correct: 'Good evening ladies and gentlemen. In the past, a man did not use a foreign tongue to speak to his own people'.

The speaker is someone addressing a gathering of people, and first he greets them. In the wrong example he immediately afterwards says, 'In those days . . .'. Only use 'In those days' when some indication of a past time has already been given:

> My father was born in 1921. In those days, communications between one part of the country and another were very slow.

153 Wrong use of **these**

Wrong: His greed, his boastfulness, his lack of manners – all these made me dislike him.

Correct: His greed, his boastfulness, his lack of manners – all this *or* all these things made me dislike him.

'This' but not 'these' can be used as a pronoun meaning the total of many different things. See also number 587 for the difference between 'this' and 'these'.

154 Wrong use of **one**

Wrong: I was hurrying across the road when I fell down one hole.

Correct: I was hurrying across the road when I fell down a hole.

Wrong: While driving through the village I accidentally ran over one pig.

Correct: While driving through the village I accidentally ran over a pig.

In both examples the 'oneness' does not need to be emphasized, so it is enough to say 'a hole', 'a pig'. To say 'one hole' implies that it is possible to fall down two holes at once, which is very unlikely in fact. Use 'one' when drawing a contrast with another number or group, for example:

> One passenger was killed; the rest were severely injured.

Here it would be wrong to say

A passenger was killed; the rest were severely injured.

A certain should be used to introduce someone or something of a definite identity which is nevertheless unknown:

Wrong: I dismissed him for a reason *or* for one reason, but I will not tell you about it yet.

Correct: I dismissed him for a certain reason, but I will not tell you about it yet.

'A' can however be used instead of 'a certain' when introducing the topic of conversation:

There was a man who had five beautiful daughters.

155 January the 5th: cardinal numbers wrongly used

Speaker A says: 'Today is the third of January; when did you say you are returning?' Speaker B is to reply.

Wrong: 'On the five.'
Correct: 'On the fifth.'

Whenever the word 'the' appears in a date, an *ordinal* number ('first', 'second', 'third', 'fourth', etc.) must follow.

Other errors

156 Unnecessary use of **any**

Wrong: There are no any decent eating-places in this town.

Correct: There are no *or* There aren't any decent eating-places in this town.

Wrong: That is all; I have no any other thing to say.

Correct: That is all; I have nothing else to say *or* I haven't anything else to say.

157 Wrong use of **cardinal numbers** after the verb '**be**'

Wrong: A: How many of you went to the cinema?
        B: We were three.
Correct: A: How many of you went to the cinema?
        B: There were three of us.

Wrong: The actors taking part in the play were fifteen.
Correct: There were fifteen actors taking part in the play.

158 Wrong use of **much** after the verb '**be**'

Wrong: Banjo complained that the noise was too much.
Correct: Banjo complained that the noise was too loud
        or that there was too much noise.

159 Wrong position of **numbers**

Wrong: You must find other five pictures to go with
        these three.
Correct: You must find five other pictures to go with
        these three.

Wrong: More fifteen students entered the school in the
        second term.
Correct: Fifteen more students entered the school in
        the second term.

160 Wrong use of **much of**

Wrong: You are making too much of noise.
Correct: You are making too much noise.

Wrong: It gives me much of pleasure to be with you.
Correct: It gives me much pleasure *or* great pleasure to
        be with you.

'Much' is followed by 'of' when it means 'a large part' of
something:

>   I spend much of *or* I spend a large part of my
>   time signing applications.
>   He found that much of the land had been sold.

161 **Of** wrongly omitted after **plenty**

Wrong: There are plenty rich farms in this area.

Correct: There are plenty of rich farms in this area.

'Plenty' is followed by 'of' before a noun; it can be used by itself only when no noun follows:

> He asked whether there were any rich farms in this area, and I said there were plenty.

162 **Of** wrongly omitted after **the rest**

Wrong: Sule and Hassan were suspended; the rest students were let off.

Correct: Sule and Hassan were suspended; the rest of the students *or* the other students were let off.

If it has already been made clear that Sule and Hassan are members of a group (of students, for example), then this sentence is also correct:

> Sule and Hassan were suspended; the rest *or* the others were let off.

Wrong: The rest important gases will be treated in a separate chapter.

Correct: The rest of the *or* The remaining *or* The remainder of the important gases will be treated in a separate chapter.

In the last example, 'remaining' or 'remainder of the' is appropriately used instead of 'rest of the' if the great majority of the gases have already been treated, and only a few remain.

163 Demonstratives and possessives wrongly used together

Wrong: I see a great future for this our country.

Correct: I see a great future for this country of ours.

Wrong: How do you propose to entertain those your guests?

Correct: How do you propose to entertain those guests of yours?

Now do Exercises 14 and 15.

5 Pronouns

Pronouns function as nouns or noun phrases. They can be classified into Subject and Object Personal Pronouns (*I, you, he, she, it, we, they; me, him, her, us, them*); Possessive Pronouns (*mine, yours, his,* etc.); Reflexive Pronouns (*myself, yourself, himself,* etc.); Interrogative or Question Pronouns (*who? what? which? whoever?* etc.); Quantifiers (*something, anything, everything, somebody, anybody, everybody; someone, anyone, everyone,* together with the Quantifiers listed at the top of Chapter 4); Negative Pronouns (*no one, nothing, nobody, none*); Relative Pronouns (*who, whom, which, that*); and a few others. This is roughly the order in which the errors below are treated. For some other references to personal pronouns, see page 205.

Many of the errors listed here are very elementary. They may not be a barrier to understanding, but they produce doubts about the writer's or speaker's competence in English.

164 **He** and **she** confused
Wrong: Did you see my sister? He went out just now.
Correct: Did you see my sister? She went out just now.

This is a notably elementary mistake, but it may be easy to make if your first language does not have separate masculine and feminine pronouns.

165 Redundant subject pronoun
Wrong: My father he works for a mining company.
Correct: My father works for a mining company.

166 **Person** wrongly used instead of **you**
Wrong: Snakes can kill person *or* human being.
Correct: Snakes can kill a person *or* a human being *or* human beings *or* you.

'Person' cannot be used in the singular without an article. 'You' here is quite correct, meaning not 'you' in particular, the person spoken to, but 'human beings in general'. Likewise:

> You have to be careful not to omit your name when writing cheques.

This is not advice given to a particular person. Its meaning could be expressed also as follows:

> One has to be careful not to omit one's name when writing cheques.

But the repetition of 'one' makes the sentence clumsy. Avoid using 'one' as a personal pronoun.

167 It has wrongly used instead of there is/are

Wrong: It has too many chairs in this room.
Correct: There are too many chairs in this room.

When the words 'in this room' are used we cannot also say 'it has', since 'it' would not refer to anything. We could only say 'it has' if the room had been mentioned in a previous sentence:

> I like this room. It has a fine view over the mountains.

168 Wrong use of it with remains

Wrong: All the other jobs have been done. It remains only the carburettor.
Correct: All the other jobs have been done. Only the carburettor remains. *or* There remains only the carburettor.

You can sometimes use 'it remains' before *to* and a verb:

> It remains only to service the carburettor.

But never use 'it remains' before a noun phrase.

169 It's mine, etc.

Wrong: A: Whose is this umbrella? B: It's for me.

Correct: A: Whose is this umbrella? B:It's mine.

Use the possessive pronouns (mine, yours, etc.) to indicate ownership.

170 A friend of mine
Wrong: I would like you to meet a friend of me *or* a friend to me.
Correct: I would like you to meet a friend of mine *or* one of my friends.

Wrong: If I did that, I wouldn't be a friend of him.
Correct: If I did that, I wouldn't be a friend of his.

171 Wrong use of **themselves**
Wrong: Though they are brother and sister, they do not love themselves.
Correct: Though they are brother and sister, they do not love each other.

Wrong: Unselfishness means that we should love ourselves.
Correct: Unselfishness means that we should love one another.

The second wrong example is a logical contradiction.

172 Myself and by myself confused
Wrong: I will kiss her by myself.
Correct: I will kiss her myself.

The use of 'by' before 'myself' means 'without any aid from anyone else', which is surely not the meaning intended. The speaker surely means that since others have kissed her, he also will kiss her. Use 'by myself' like this:

> I want to go for a walk by myself, so you do something else.

173 Wrong use of **a** before **somebody**
Wrong: He is a dirty somebody – he seldom takes a bath.

Correct: He is a dirty person – he seldom takes a bath.

In general, determiners (e.g. 'a') cannot be used before pronouns (e.g. 'somebody'). Use a noun (e.g. 'person') instead of a pronoun after a determiner.

174 Wrong use of object pronoun in relative clauses

Wrong: They went to see the palace, which the King had built it many decades earlier.

Correct: They went to see the palace, which the King had built many decades earlier.

Wrong: He gave me some yams, which I put them in the boot of my car.

Correct: He gave me some yams, which I put in the boot of my car.

175 **What** and **that** confused

Wrong: I was dismayed by all what I heard.
Correct: I was dismayed by all that I heard.

Always say 'all that', never 'all what'.

176 **Whose**

Wrong: People who their power is great should use it wisely.

Correct: People whose power is great should use it wisely.

Never use 'who' followed by a possessive.

177 Redundant subject pronoun after **who**

Wrong: The girl who she went with you is my sister.
Correct: The girl who went with you is my sister.

'Who' is the subject of the verb 'went'; it is impossible to put in another subject, 'she'.

178 The relative pronoun after prepositions

Wrong: The man who we sat together on the plane is a Minister.

Correct: The man who sat with me on the plane is a
Minister.

It is quite permissible in modern spoken English to omit
the relative pronoun, as in the second of the correct forms
in the example. Likewise we can say:

The house I live in is built of stone.
The person I gave the money to said his name
was Audu.

In more formal English we would say:

The house in which I live is built of stone.
The person to whom I gave the money said his
name was Audu.

179 **Such** wrongly used

Wrong: It was a most horrible accident. I have never
seen such before.

Correct: It was a most horrible accident. I have never
seen such an accident *or* I have never seen one
like it *or* I have never seen anything like it
before.

'Such' cannot stand on its own as a pronoun except when
it comes before some part of the verb 'be'. For example:

He breathed his last and departed from this life.
Such is the fate of all mankind.

180 **As such** wrongly used

Wrong: The businessman was found guilty of fraud; as
such, he was fined ₦5000.

Correct: The businessman was found guilty of fraud; as
a result, he was fined ₦5000.

'As such' is an important-sounding little phrase which can
be over-used. It means 'in one's capacity as' something
just mentioned, but here it is redundant. It adds nothing
to say 'in his capacity of being found guilty'. 'As such'
could be used correctly like this:

A teacher used to be considered someone of exceptional wisdom. As such, he was held in high honour.

Now do Exercises 16 and 17.

6 Verbs

Incorrect Verb Forms

Students of this book should already be familiar with these general rules concerning the formation of verbs:

1 The form of a verb given in the dictionary is also known as the INFINITIVE, and also as the IMPERATIVE, used to express a command: e.g., dictionary form and infinitive, *go*; imperative, *Go!*

2 The same form serves as the Present Simple Tense for all persons except the third person singular: e.g., *I go, you go, we go, they go*. The third person singular has an added *-s* or *-es*: *he goes, she goes, it goes*. For 'person', see page 205.

3 The endings *-ing* and *-d* or *-ed* are added to the dictionary form to produce PARTICIPLES: e.g. *loving* (Present), *loved* (Past).

4 Most verbs are REGULAR: that is, the Past Tense and the Past Participle are formed by adding *-d* or *-ed* to the dictionary form. But there are also a number of IRREGULAR verbs, which change in other ways. A list of common irregular verbs is given on pages 222–7.

5 Various AUXILIARIES (*be, am, is, are, was, were, being, been, have, has, had, having, do, does, did*) combine with the participles according to certain rules to produce many other verb forms. In general these are known as TENSES. A list of these appears on page 204.

Failure to observe these rules account for a great many common errors in verb formation. Most of these are to be counted elementary errors; the advanced student should therefore make a particular effort to avoid committing them.

Verbs are found in statement form, or question form, or imperative form, and for each of these there is a negative form. This section is confined to the statement form; wrong question or negative forms are treated in the next section.

181 Present Simple Tense: Wrong Omission of -s (Third Person Singular)

Wrong: She speak with a strange accent.
Correct: She speaks with a strange accent.

Wrong: The cutlass belong to me.
Correct: The cutlass belongs to me.

Wrong: It seem that he has returned.
Correct: It seems that he has returned.

182 Present Simple Tense: wrong use of -s in the Plural

Wrong: They knows everything about you.
Correct: They know everything about you.

Wrong: We likes reading.
Correct: We like reading.

Wrong: These newspapers only carries propaganda.
Correct: These newspapers only carry propaganda.

Wrong: The muscles of the leg controls the ankle and the foot.
Correct: The muscles of the leg control the ankle and the foot.

Note that -*s* must be added to nouns to make them plural, but never to verbs.

183 Stative verbs wrongly given continuous forms

Wrong: I am knowing that you are my best friend.
Correct: I know that you are my best friend.

Wrong: I am liking the way you address him.
Correct: I like the way you address him.

Wrong: This hat was not belonging to you.
Correct: This hat did not belong to you.

Wrong: I am seeing the ship on the horizon.
Correct: I can see the ship on the horizon.

The verbs used in these examples – *know, like, belong, see* – are members of a much-used group often called STATIVE VERBS. The main thing to note about them is that normally they have *no continuous forms*. Instead of the Present Continuous use the Present Simple, instead of the Past Continuous use the Past Simple, etc. A fuller list of these verbs is given on page 207; also see number 210.

184 Wrong omission of **am, is, are**, etc. in Continuous Forms

Wrong: My brother working at a tyre factory now.
Correct: My brother ⎰ is working ⎱ at a tyre factory now.
⎱ works ⎰

Wrong: They finding it hard to forgive you.
Correct: They ⎰ are finding ⎱ it hard to forgive you.
⎱ find ⎰

185 Wrong forms of **hit, split, cast**, etc.

Wrong: She seized the pestle and hitted me.
Correct: She seized the pestle and hit me.

Wrong: The resolution was passed, and they splitted off from the Party.
Correct: The resolution was passed, and they split off from the Party.

Wrong: He casted his vote in favour of the motion.
Correct: He cast his vote in favour of the motion.

See pages 222–7. 'Split', 'hit', and 'cast' are irregular verbs because all their parts are the same: *hit – hit – hit*; *split – split – split*; *cast – cast – cast*. Other common verbs whose parts are all the same are 'cut' and 'let'.

186 Wrong forms of **send, lend, spend**, etc.

Wrong: Yaro complained of toothache, so I send him home.
Correct: Yaro complained of toothache, so I sent him home.

Wrong: It was good of you to lent me that money last
week.
Correct: It was good of you to lend me that money last
week.

Wrong: He has spend the last three years in exile.
Correct: He has spent the last three years in exile.

These verbs are irregular because the final -*d* changes to
-*t* for the Past Simple and the Past Participle: *send – sent
– sent*; *lend – lent – lent*; *spend – spent – spent*.

187 Wrong forms of **go**
Wrong: I gone to see my mother last week.
Correct: I went to see my mother last week.

Wrong: The match is over; the spectators have all went
home.
Correct: The match is over; the spectators have all gone
home.

'Go' is a notably irregular verb.

188 Wrong forms of **bear**
Wrong: She born him three children in two years.
Correct: She bore *or* She has borne him three children
in two years.

Wrong: He did not know she was unable to born
children.
Correct: He did not know she was unable to bear
children.

The parts of this verb are: *bear* (basic form or infinitive);
bore (past simple); *born* or *borne* (past participle). Of the
past participle alternatives, 'borne' is used to make up
perfect tenses; 'born' is used with 'was', 'were', etc., to
make up the passive.

189 Wrong use of **-ed** after an infinitive (1)
Wrong: Alhaji Yahaya decided to travelled to the
Middle East.

Correct: Alhaji Yahaya decided to travel to the Middle East.

Wrong: The Registrar tried to sent you a telegram.
Correct: The Registrar tried to send you a telegram.

Wrong: The villagers wanted to extended the boundaries of their land.
Correct: The villagers wanted to extend the boundaries of their land.

The use of 'to' in these examples shows that the verb which follows is an infinitive. Nothing may be added to an infinitive in any circumstances.

190 Wrong use of -ed after an infinitive (2)
Wrong: He made me followed him to the library.
Correct: He made me follow him to the library.

Wrong: I saw him threw the refuse into the water.
Correct: I saw him throw the refuse into the water.

In these examples 'follow' and 'throw' are also infinitives, though without any preceding 'to'. They form part of the pattern that follows 'made' and 'saw' respectively. (See page 129.)

191 Wrong use of the plural with **much**
Wrong: Much have been said about Shaka's achievements.
Correct: 1 Much has been said about Shaka's achievements.
2 Many things have been said about Shaka's achievements.

'Much' must be treated as singular, though it may have plural meaning.

192 Wrong use of plural verbs with uncountable nouns
Wrong: 'What are the importance of agriculture?' he asked.

Correct: 'What is the importance of agriculture?' he
asked.

When the subject of a verb is an uncountable noun, the
verb must be singular. In the above example, if the
speaker wants to emphasize that he is calling for several
points to be made, the sentence would have to be put in
a different way:

'In what ways is agriculture important?' he
asked.

193 Omission of Past Participle **-d** or **-ed** in Perfect Tenses

Wrong: I have just open a bank account.
Correct: I have just opened a bank account.

Wrong: He has at last finish building his house.
Correct: He has at last finished building his house.

Wrong: She said she had try her best to see you.
Correct: She said she had tried her best to see you.

194 Omission of Past Participle **-d** or **-ed** in the Passive

Wrong: I am much influence in my ideas by my
father.
Correct: I am much influenced in my ideas by my
father.

Wrong: News of the coup has just been announce over
the radio.
Correct: News of the coup has just been announced
over the radio.

Wrong: The names of the applicants were not mention.
Correct: The names of the applicants were not
mentioned.

This error is very similar to numbers 62–3, discussed
under adjectives. In all these examples it can be easy both
to omit the final -*d*, both in speaking and writing; and,

again, its omission is an indication of carelessness or imperfect learning.

Wrong Formation of Questions and Negatives

The following general rules are expected to be already known and correctly applied:

1 To form the question and negative forms of their Present Simple and Past Simple Tenses, all verbs (except auxiliaries) make use of the auxiliary verb *do*. The verb with which *do* is used loses any endings that go with the statement form.

2 To form direct questions, the subject of the verb changes places with the first auxiliary verb that follows the subject: *I have . . .* becomes *Have* I. . .?, etc. This changing of places is called inversion.

3 To form negatives, the word *not* is placed after the first auxiliary verb that follows the subject: *I have* becomes *I have not*, etc. In less formal writing, such as personal letters, this *not* may be written *n't*, and is then joined to the auxiliary that comes before it: *haven't, aren't* etc.

Common errors include the misuse of *do, does,* and *did*; the failure to drop *-s* and *-ed* when the parts of *do* are used; the non-formation of proper 'tag' questions that can be added to statements; and non-inversion when inversion is required.

195 Wrong use of **-s** in Present Simple questions

Wrong: A: Does he understands Yoruba? B: Yes, he understands Yoruba very well.

Correct: A: Does he understand Yoruba? B: Yes, he understands Yoruba very well.

Wrong: A: Does your sister knows my mother? B: Yes, she knows your mother quite well.

Correct: A: Does your sister know my mother? B: Yes, she knows your mother quite well.

Wrong: A: How far does your land extends? B: It extends only as far as that tree.

Correct: A: How far does your land extend? B: It extends only as far as that tree.

As the examples show, no -s must be used after the verb in the question; but it must be used in the answer, which is in statement form.

196 Wrong use of **-s** in Present Simple negative forms

Wrong: She doesn't feels sleepy any more.
Correct: She doesn't feel sleepy any more.

Wrong: They don't expects anyone to come.
Correct: They don't expect anyone to come.

Wrong: He doesn't believes what you say.
Correct: He doesn't believe what you say.

197 Wrong use of **-ed** in Past Simple questions

Wrong: A: Did he arrived late? B: No, he arrived quite early.
Correct: A: Did he arrive late? B: No, he arrived quite early.

Wrong: A: Who did you supported? B: I supported Mr Gatuma.
Correct: A: Who did you support? B: I supported Mr Gatuma.

The error is really that of using the statement form of the Past Simple Tense in the question form. Note also

Wrong: A: What did he bought? B: He bought a new radio.
Correct: A: What did he buy? B: He bought a new radio.

Wrong: A: Where did she found it? B: She found it in the office.
Correct: A: Where did she find it? B: She found it in the office.

198 Wrong use of **-ed** in Past Simple negatives

Wrong: He didn't kicked the ball hard enough.
Correct: He didn't kick the ball hard enough.

Once again, the error is that of using the statement form of the Past Simple Tense, as in these other examples:

Wrong: The tree swayed but it didn't fell.
Correct: The tree swayed but it didn't fall.

Wrong: She didn't took the tablets she collected.
Correct: She didn't take the tablets she collected.

199 **Did** wrongly used in questions

Example 1 A: My vegetables are growing nicely.
Wrong: B: Did it always rain much at this time?
Correct: B: Does it always rain much at this time?

Example 2 A: I play volley-ball for the school.
Wrong: B. Did you play soccer for the school also?
Correct: B: Do you play soccer for the school also?

200 **Is, are** wrongly used in questions

Wrong: Are you go to see the last festival we held?
Correct: Did you go to see the last festival we held?

Wrong: Is she take her child to the hospital yesterday?
Correct: Did she take her child to the hospital yesterday?

This error is a very serious one. Not only does the speaker not know that *did* must be used here; he also shows that he does not know how to use *are* and *is* as auxiliaries. As auxiliaries, *are* and *is* must be followed by a verb ending in *-ing*.

201 Tag questions wrongly formed

Wrong: Banjo is coming tomorrow, isn't it?
Correct: Banjo is coming tomorrow, isn't he?

Wrong: They were advised to apply, isn't it?
Correct: They were advised to apply, weren't they?

Wrong: She dresses magnificently, isn't it?
Correct: She dresses magnificently, doesn't she?

Wrong: They shot two elephants, isn't it?
Correct: They shot two elephants, didn't they?

Wrong: You will be there, isn't it?
Correct: You will be there, won't you?

Tag questions are so called because they are 'tagged on' or added at the end of a statement. Do not use 'isn't it' every time you want to add such a question. As the examples show, the verb used in the 'tag' must match the verb used in the statement, and once again the auxiliary *do* must be introduced. This is one way in which English is quite unlike other languages.

202 Echo questions

Wrong: A: A fight started. B: Is that?
Correct: A: A fight started. B: Is that so? *or* Did it?

Wrong: A: Scorpions can kill. B: Is that?
Correct: A: Scorpions can kill. B: Is that so? *or* Can they?

Echo questions are like tag questions in the way they are formed, and an echo question is used by one person to express surprise at another person's statement. 'Is that?' is always wrong; but also try to avoid using 'Is that so?' on every occasion, though it is marked as correct here.

203 Non-inversion of subject and verb in direct questions

Wrong: 'Where you went to?' my friend asked me.
Correct: 'Where did you go to?' my friend asked me.

Wrong: 'What programme you did see last night?' I asked.
Correct: 'What programme did you see last night?' I asked.

Wrong: 'When your son will graduate?' she asked me.
Correct: 'When will your son graduate?' she asked me.

204 Wrong inversion of subject and verb in indirect questions

Wrong: He asked me how much did I want to pay.
Correct: He asked me how much I wanted to pay.

Wrong: I asked him when would he have the time to interview me.
Correct: I asked him when he would have the time to interview me.

Wrong: I wanted to know what was the time.
Correct: I wanted to know what the time was.

205 Wrong repetition of verb in answers
Wrong: A: Did you give him the key? B: No, I didn't give.
Correct: A: Did you give him the key? B: No, I didn't. *or* No, I didn't give it to him.

Wrong: A: Does she like the new house? B: Yes, she likes.
Correct: A: Does she like the new house? B: Yes, she does. *or* Yes, she likes it.

206 Non-inversion of subject and auxiliary verb after **never, no sooner, not only**
Wrong: Never we agreed that you should become Treasurer.
Correct: Never did we agree that you should become Treasurer.

Wrong: No sooner he had stood up than the applause started.
Correct: No sooner had he stood up than the applause started.

Wrong: Not only he went to Australia, he visited some of the remotest areas there.
Correct: Not only did he go to Australia, he visited some of the remotest areas there.

Note that in these examples *Never, No sooner,* and *Not only* come at the beginning of the sentence. The remaining two errors in this section also concern inversion, though not in question forms.

207 Non-inversion of subject and verb after **so, neither, nor**

Wrong: A: I know how to swim. B: So I do.
Correct: A: I know how to swim. B: So do I. *or* I do, too.

Wrong: A: I don't like smoking. B: Neither I do.
Correct: A: I don't like smoking. B: Neither do I. *or* Nor do I. *or* I don't, either.

208 Non-use of **so am I**, etc.

Wrong: A: I always take a siesta in the afternoon. B: Likewise myself.
Correct: A: I always take a siesta in the afternoon. B: So do I. *or* I do, too.

Wrong: A: I'm getting very tired of him. B: Likewise myself.
Correct: A: I'm getting very tired of him. B: So am I. *or* I am, too.

Wrong: A: I can play ten games without a rest. B: Likewise myself.
Correct: A: I can play ten games without a rest. B: So can I. *or* I can, too.

The same kind of advice applies here as in number 201. 'Likewise myself' is not a bad mistake, or is not even a mistake at all from the point of view of grammatical structure; but it is a lazy way of avoiding the use of *So* followed by an auxiliary.

Now do exercise 30.

Verb Forms misused

You were reminded in the introduction to this chapter on page 54 that auxiliaries and participles combine with the dictionary form of a verb to produce various other forms known in general as tenses. They are distinguished from one another by Tense (Present, Past), Aspect (Simple, Continuous or Progressive,

Perfect), and Voice (Active, Passive). A maximum of 14 tenses can be formed for each verb (excluding question and negative forms of these tenses); 8 active and 6 passive, though some of them are much more widely used than others. For every given situation there is an appropriate tense. Very generally:

TENSE: The PRESENT refers to present and sometimes to future time; the PAST to past time.

ASPECT: The SIMPLE aspect refers to events that happen once or often, the CONTINUOUS or PROGRESSIVE to events that take place continuously over a period, and the PERFECT to an event that began in the past and continues into the present, or to an event that happened in the past but had an effect that is still felt in the present.

VOICE: The noun or pronoun subject of an ACTIVE verb performs an action (*He loves*); the noun or pronoun subject of a PASSIVE verb is acted upon (*He is loved*).

Making the right choice of tense is a fertile source of error, perfect tenses giving particular difficulty. The passive also presents problems, chiefly by not being used when it ought to be used. It is widely used in English, especially in the kind of abstract and technical English to which students in higher institutions and people in professional occupations are exposed.

209 Simple forms wrongly used instead of Continuous forms

Wrong: Mary does the housework at present; she will not be long.

Correct: Mary is doing the housework at present; she will not be long.

Wrong: The goats make a lot of noise today.

Correct: The goats are making a lot of noise today.

Wrong: Look at him! He drinks the entire bottle of whisky I placed in front of him.

Correct: Look at him! He is drinking the entire bottle of whisky I placed in front of him.

Wrong: I travelled to Kisumu when the tyre burst.
Correct: I was travelling to Kisumu when the tyre burst.

Sometimes both the simple and continuous forms are correct. This is true, for example, of verbs expressing emotion or sensation:

> I expect him back any time from now.
> I am expecting him back any time from now.
>
> I feel cold.
> I am feeling cold.

210 Wrong use of the Continuous forms of **have**
Wrong: A: What's the matter with you? B: I'm having malaria.
Correct: A: What's the matter with you? B: I have malaria.

The continuous forms of 'have' cannot be used when 'have' denotes a state or a condition rather than an action. But it is correct to say:

> I'm having a bath.
> I'm having a new pair of trousers made.

211 Present Simple wrongly used instead of the Present Perfect
Wrong: I am here since one o'clock.
Correct: I have been here since one o'clock.

Wrong: Nwankwo is working in Benin since 1970.
Correct: Nwankwo has been working in Benin since 1970.

Wrong: They are missing for the past two weeks.
Correct: They have been missing for the past two weeks.

When 'since' and 'for' are used in time phrases, and past time is indicated, use the Present Perfect.

212 Present Perfect wrongly used instead of Past Simple

Wrong: I have seen his wife several times last week.
Correct: I saw his wife several times last week.

Wrong: The Organization of African Unity has been set up in 1963.
Correct: The Organization of African Unity was set up in 1963.

Wrong: His second burial has taken place in January.
Correct: His second burial took place in January.

When a definite point of past time is indicated and not a period, use the Past Simple.

213 Past Perfect wrongly used

Wrong: It had been reported to me that some of you are in possession of hemp. You will surrender it.
Correct: It has been reported to me that some of you are in possession of hemp. You will surrender it.

Wrong: The latest news is that all the documents had been destroyed in last week's fire.
Correct: The latest news is that all the documents were destroyed in last week's fire.

Wrong: A long time ago, a mighty civilization had flourished in Egypt.
Correct: A long time ago, a mighty civilization flourished in Egypt.

The misuse of the Past Perfect is a very common error, which can cause misunderstanding. The essential thing to note is that it is not to be used when you just wish to indicate that something happened a very long time ago. It is normally used when two past events happening at different times are referred to in the same statement. The Past Perfect is then used for the earlier event, and the Past Simple for the later event. For example:

He *did not meet* them because they *had left*.
Past Simple   Past Perfect

He *asked* me why I *had divorced* her.
Past Simple   Past Perfect

If the Past Perfect is the only verb used in a sentence, the Past Simple will usually be found in a neighbouring sentence:

> My father died in 1980. He had seen many changes during his life.

214 Present Perfect wrongly used instead of Past Perfect

Wrong: Long before the Arabs arrived, a mighty civilization has already flourished in Egypt.

Correct: Long before the Arabs arrived, a mighty civilization had already flourished in Egypt.

This error is the reverse of the previous one.

215 Emphatic **do** wrongly used

Wrong: Coal is largely carbon, and diamonds do come from carbon too.

Correct: Coal is largely carbon, and diamonds come from carbon too.

Wrong: She described her adventures in great detail; at the end all the audience did clap.

Correct: She described her adventures in great detail; at the end all the audience clapped.

Besides its use in questions and negatives, *do* (*does*, *did*) can sometimes be used to give emphasis to statements. But in the above examples emphasis is unnecessary or meaningless. *Do* is normally used by one speaker to affirm strongly something which is denied by another speaker. For example:

> I did take the test, even though I was marked 'absent'.

216 Wrong choice of tense in the passive (1)

Wrong: Air was composed of several gases, but nitrogen accounts for more than 75%.

Correct: Air is composed of several gases, but nitrogen accounts for more than 75%.

Wrong: The only elements which were attracted by a magnet are iron, cobalt, and nickel.

Correct: The only elements which are attracted by a magnet are iron, cobalt, and nickel.

217 Wrong choice of tense in the passive (2)

Wrong: About the year 1400 it is decided *or* it was been decided to build another city elsewhere.

Correct: About the year 1400 it was decided to build another city elsewhere.

Errors 216 and 217 may be due simply to failure to form tenses in the passive correctly. In 216, the Present Simple passive is needed: laws of natural science are being stated. The rule for the formation of the Present Simple passive is Present Simple of *be* + past participle of main verb (*composed, attracted*). In 217 the Past Simple passive is needed to describe a historical event, and the rule here is: Past Simple of *be* and past participle of main verb.

218 Active forms wrongly used: **situate**

Wrong: The town situates on a railway line.

Correct: The town is situated on a railway line.

'Situate' is more often found in the passive than in the active. It is correctly used in the active like this:

> The Government decided to situate the new capital right in the centre of the country.

219 Active forms wrongly used: **marry**

Wrong: My brother is marrying three wives; each has given him a son.

Correct: My brother has three wives; each has given him a son.

The active continuous forms of 'marry' cannot be used to mean 'have taken in marriage', 'be married to'. The active continuous forms can only be used to describe the action of the person who performs the rite of marriage for the two parties concerned:

> The priest is marrying three separate couples today.

The *passive* forms of 'marry' are much more common:

> They have been married for twenty years.
> She was married to a man twenty years her senior.

It is also correct to use 'get married' for the act of becoming married:

> He got married at quite an advanced age.

220 Active forms wrongly used: **hold**

Wrong: I will attend the convention holding at Enugu on the 29th.

Correct: I will attend the convention to be held *or* being held at Enugu on the 29th.

Wrong: I shall be disappointed if the meeting does not hold.

Correct: I shall be disappointed if the meeting is not held.

'Hold' when it is used in the active and means 'conduct' (a meeting, etc.) must usually be followed by an object; the object can also be the subject of a passive verb. The use of the active without an object is confined to legal use, and sounds archaic in everyday English.

221 Active forms wrongly used: **suppose**

Wrong: You suppose to write your registration number.

Correct: You are supposed to write your registration number.

The idea is that you are under an obligation; and this is what 'you are supposed' means. The active form 'suppose' means 'imagine', 'think', for example:

I suppose the case will soon be concluded.

222 Active forms wrongly used: **wound**

Wrong: I hear Obi was knocked down; did he wound?
Correct: I hear Obi was knocked down; was he wounded?

'Wound' can be a noun or a verb. As a verb it can be used both in the active and in the passive, but the active forms cannot be used without an object following. That is to say, the verb 'wound' means 'give someone a wound'.

223 Non-use of **have** + noun + participle

Wrong: He went to the barber's to cut his hair.
Correct: He went to the barber's to have his hair cut.

The incorrect sentence means that he went to the barber's, but intended to use the scissors on his hair himself.

Wrong: I must go to Africa Motors to repair my car.
Correct: I must go to Africa Motors to have my car repaired.

I would hardly take my car to Africa Motors if I were going to do the repairs myself, as the incorrect sentence implies.

224 **Sleep** wrongly used:

Wrong: A: Where is Femi? B: He has slept.
Correct: A: Where is Femi? B: He has gone to bed. *or* He is asleep. *or* He is sleeping.

The verb 'sleep' does not mean 'fall asleep' or 'go to bed to sleep', but 'be in a state of sleep'. The perfect tense of the verb could be used like this:

So you are awake at last! Do you know you have slept for fourteen hours?

Modals wrongly formed and misused

Modals, or modal verbs, or modal auxiliaries, are a small group of very important words: *will, would, shall, should, can, could, may, might, must, ought to, have to, am to* (*is to, are to*, etc.), *used to, need, dare*. They are auxiliaries because they are found before main verbs, and cannot be used on their own. Other points to note are:

1 Modals have no endings. (But *have to* can change to *had to* or *having to; am to* can also change, as shown above.)
2 Modals cannot be preceded by other modals. (*Have to* is again an exception.)
3 The main verb used after the modal is the dictionary or infinitive form, with no endings.
4 Some modals go in pairs, one in a pair acting as a present tense form, the other as a past tense form: *will* (present) and *would* (past); *shall* (present) and *should* (past); *can* (present) and *could* (past); *may* (present) and *might* (past).

Modals are used to express a speaker's attitudes: prediction, desire, permission, insistence, etc. Obviously the wrong choice of modal can completely alter the way a speaker wishes to be understood; errors in the use of modals are therefore the cause of much misunderstanding. The errors shown here include malformation of modal + main verb phrases, and the wrong choice of one modal instead of another.

225 Wrong use of **to** after modals

> *Wrong:* You must to bring two goats with you.
> *Correct:* You must bring two goats with you.

> *Wrong:* I could not to find my way to the beach.
> *Correct:* I could not find my way to the beach.

Among the modals it is only after 'ought', 'used', and 'have/has/had' that 'to' can be used:

> We ought to write him a letter of thanks.
> He went bankrupt and had to sell all his property.

226 **Would** wrongly used instead of **will**

Wrong: Our electricity would be restored tomorrow. The Manager has promised.

Correct: Our electricity will be restored tomorrow. The Manager has promised.

Wrong: Please note: only those who submit their names would receive the allowance.

Correct: Please note: only those who submit their names will receive the allowance.

Using 'would' here implies some uncertainty, or some condition. Instead, the speaker in each example predicts the future with certainty. Also see number 247.

227 **Shall** wrongly used instead of **will**

Wrong: I trust that he shall be back before Tuesday.

Correct: I trust that he will be back before Tuesday.

Wrong: You shall provide me with the statistics on my next visit.

Correct: You will provide me with the statistics on my next visit.

When used with second and third persons, 'shall' expresses the strong insistence of the speaker. In the first example, the speaker cannot at the same time express insistence and confidence ('I trust'). In the second example, the speaker wants to give an order, but this order is given by 'will'; nothing is gained by substituting 'shall' for 'will'.

Here is an example of the correct use of 'shall' with second or third persons:

> You shall get that prize; no one can take away your right to it.

For 'persons', see page 205.

228 **Will** wrongly used

Wrong: So you are going to the market? You will buy me some meat.

> *Correct:* So you are going to the market? Could you
> buy me some meat? *or* I'd like you to buy me
> some meat.

'You will . . .' often expresses an order or even a threat given by one person to another; it does not sound polite. 'Could you' or 'I'd like you to' expresses the polite request which is surely being made in the above example.
'You will . . .' could be used like this:

> You will stop writing when I say 'Put down your
> pens'.

229 Should wrongly used

Wrong: I hope he should be here before darkness falls.
Correct: I hope he will be here before darkness falls.

'Should' expresses obligation or necessity:

> I said he should be here before darkness falls.

In the incorrect example, one cannot hope and impose an obligation on somebody at the same time.

230 Like and would like

Wrong: I like to receive those plans you promised me
now.
Correct: I would like *or* I should like to receive those
plans you promised me now.

'Would like' ('should like' is an alternative for the first person) expresses a polite request for something at a particular time. 'Like' just expresses a general preference:

> I like receiving presents when I don't expect
> them.

231 Can and be able to wrongly used together

Wrong: If you can be able to meet him, he will put
you through.
Correct: If you can meet him *or* If you are able to meet
him, he will put you through.

'Can' and 'be able to' have the same meaning, so they cannot be used together.

232 Can and be possible wrongly used together

Wrong: It cannot be possible for you to see the doctor today.

Correct: It is not possible for you to see *or* You cannot see the doctor today.

'Can' and 'be possible' have the same meaning, so they cannot be used together.

233 Wrong use of may

Wrong: May the honourable members please come and sign their names.

Correct: 1 Would the honourable members please come and sign their names?

2 The honourable members are requested to come and sign their names.

'May' followed by the subject only expresses a request when the subject is 'I' or 'we', for example:

May I (please) borrow this book?

Otherwise it expresses a wish:

May you prosper in all your undertakings.
May God bless you.

234 Wrong use of you may

Wrong: You may kindly read this letter and offer your comments.

Correct: Would you kindly read this letter and offer your comments?

The use of 'kindly' here implies that the speaker wants to put a polite request to the person addressed; but 'You may . . .' does not indicate a request.

'You may . . .' could be used like this:

You may like to read this letter and offer your comments.

Here, 'may' indicates possibility. The meaning of the sentence is something like 'Possibly you will like to read this letter and offer your comments.' Sometimes also 'may' indicates permission:

> You may go now.

235 Wrong use of **might be**

Wrong: Might be he was the murderer.
Correct: Maybe he was the murderer.

There is no adverb 'might be' that can be used to correspond to 'maybe' even though the main verb in the sentence is in the Past Tense.

236 **Must** and **have to** wrongly used together

Wrong: He says you must have to settle your debt next week.
Correct: He says you must settle *or* will have to settle your debt next week.

A future obligation can be expressed by 'must' or 'will have to be', but not by a combination of the two.

237 Wrong use of **must have, might have** in time clauses

Wrong: After he might have come back *or* After he must have come back, I will give him the money.
Correct: After he comes back *or* After he has come back, I will give him the money.

Wrong: When he might have finished his speech *or* must have finished his speech, I will depart.
Correct: When he finishes his speech *or* has finished his speech, I will depart.

Wrong: As soon as you might have remembered the word *or* must have remembered the word, write it down.
Correct: As soon as you remember the word *or* have remembered the word, write it down.

'Must have' and 'might have' cannot be used in time clauses referring to the future. They are used correctly like this:

> I can hear the sound of an engine: John must have returned.
>
> He said an explosion might have taken place if the security men had not been on the alert.
>
> You might have told me you were coming – I would have sent my car to the airport!

238 Had to wrongly used

Wrong: Many people had to fall sick when the weather turned cold.

Correct: Many people fell sick when the weather turned cold.

'Had to' expresses an obligation or logical necessity in the past. In this example the people could not have been under any obligation to fall sick, nor could their falling sick have been logically necessary.

239 Can I? wrongly used

Wrong: A: You said there was beer. B: There is. Can I bring it?

Correct: A: You said there was beer. B: There is. Shall I bring it? *or* Am I to bring it?

'Can I . . .?' means that the speaker is making a personal request, which may be granted or refused:

> Can I have one of these photographs?

But the job of a waiter in a hotel – speaker 'B' in the first example – is merely to find out the wishes of a client – speaker 'A' in the example. The waiter's personal wishes have no bearing on the matter; it is of no importance if the waiter *wants* to bring beer to the client. It is with 'Shall I . . .?' or 'Am I . . .?' that one person places himself at the service of another.

Nevertheless, 'Can I . . .?' would not be wrong in this example:

You are welcome. Can I bring you a chair? *or* Shall I bring you a chair?

Here extra informality and friendliness is expressed by 'Can I . . .?' instead of 'Shall I . . .?', and this is appropriate where one friend is welcoming another, for example. 'Can I . . .?' shows there is a personal desire to satisfy the visitor.

240 Wrong Present Tense form of **used to**

Wrong: He has stopped smoking, but he still use to drink too much.

Correct: He has stopped smoking, but he still drinks too much *or* is still drinking too much.

'Used to' is a correct form indicating a habit or a routine in the past, for example:

> He used to work for the Water Board, but now he is on his own.

There is no Present Tense form 'use to'. To indicate a habit in the present, use the Present Simple or the Present Continuous Tense.

Sequence of Tenses

In the sentence *He knows that Stella likes him* two verbs are used, *knows* and *likes*. Both are in the Present Simple Tense. If the same sentence were put into the Past Simple Tense it would become *He knew that Stella liked him*. Both verbs are now in the Past Simple Tense.

This simple example illustrates an important rule about verbs, called the SEQUENCE OF TENSES: if a verb in the main clause (e.g. *He knows*) is a present tense, the verb in the *that*-clause (e.g. *that Stella likes him*) must also be a Present Tense; and if the verb in the main clause is a Past Tense (e.g. *He knew*), the verb in the *that*-clause must also be a Past Tense (e.g. *that Stella liked him*).

One important exception to this rule may be illustrated using the same example as above. This sentence is correct: *He knows that Stella liked him.* It means that Stella liked him previously, but no longer likes him, or for one reason or another is no longer one of his friends. The Past Tense is needed because what was true in the past is no longer true in the present. There are other exceptions to the rule; but it is essential first to know the rule, and practise it.

The sequence of tenses rule must also be obeyed when forming *indirect* questions, for example:

> The judge *asked* whether the accused *had* ever been in prison before.

This corresponds to the *direct question*

> 'Has the accused ever been in prison before?' asked the judge.

Here the actual words of the judge are quoted, and to indicate this inverted commas and a question mark are used.

A more detailed presentation of the Sequence of Tenses rule, including the rules for forming indirect questions from direct questions, is given on pages 210–13.

Failure to obey the rule is a frequent source of error, especially when the verb in the main clause is in a Past Tense. Obviously, to follow the rule it is necessary to know the Past Tense form of any verb, regular or irregular, and also the Past Tense of any auxiliary or modal verb.

241 Non-use of Past Tense -ed

> *Wrong:* It seems you abandon her and did not wish to see her again.
> *Correct:* It seems you abandoned her and did not wish to see her again.

> *Wrong:* I learned that you call at my place yesterday.
> *Correct:* I learned that you called at my place yesterday.

242 Non-use of Past Tense forms of irregular verbs

> *Wrong:* He said that they go to Jinja last Tuesday.
> *Correct:* He said that they went to Jinja last Tuesday.

Wrong: I was surprised that he make no attempt to prevent the riot from starting.

Correct: I was surprised that he made no attempt to prevent the riot from starting.

243 Is wrongly used instead of **was**

Wrong: John said he is in a hurry; that was why he didn't wait.

Correct: John said he was in a hurry; that was why he didn't wait.

244 Are wrongly used instead of **were**

Wrong: You knew you are told to produce one more copy; why have you not done so?

Correct: You knew you were told to produce one more copy; why have you not done so?

245 Has wrongly used instead of **had**

Wrong: In her statement to the police she said that her purse has been snatched by the young man.

Correct: In her statement to the police she said that her purse had been snatched by the young man.

The Present Perfect is wrongly used instead of the Past Perfect; see also number 214.

246 Will wrongly used instead of **would**

Wrong: He asked whether he will be allowed to see you; but you had departed for Kano.

Correct: He asked whether he would be allowed to see you; but you had departed for Kano.

Would is the Past Tense of *will*. (See page 73.)

247 Would wrongly used instead of **will**

Wrong: It has been announced that there would be a public holiday tomorrow.

Correct: It has been announced that there will be a public holiday tomorrow.

This is the opposite of the previous error. It is very like error number 226.

248 **Can** wrongly used instead of **could**

Wrong: I was sure that he cannot apply the brakes in time; that was how the accident happened.

Correct: I was sure that he could not apply the brakes in time; that was how the accident happened.

249 **Does** wrongly used instead of **did**

Wrong: I suppose the reason he does not get out his camera is simply that it was too late in the day.

Correct: I suppose the reason he did not get out his camera is simply that it was too late in the day.

250 General mixing of tenses

Finally in this section it should be noted that the Sequence of Tenses rule is not one to be observed just in sentences beginning 'He said that . . .', 'I know that . . .', 'She asked whether . . .', etc. In whole passages it is important to be consistent in the use of tenses, and not to wander haphazardly from past to present or from present to past. Stories can be told, for example, either in the present or in the past, but not in a mixture of both:

Wrong: The king of the birds told his representative to go and collect taxes from all birds. When the representative comes to the bat's house and asks him to pay the tax, the bat laughed and said, 'Have you ever seen a bird with teeth?'

Correct: 1 The king of the birds told his representative to go and collect taxes from all birds. When the representative came to the bat's house and asked him to pay the tax, the bat laughed and said, 'Have you ever seen a bird with teeth?'

Correct: 2 The king of the birds tells his representative to go and collect taxes from all birds. When the representative comes to the bat's house and asks him to pay the tax, the bat laughs and says, 'Have you ever seen a bird with teeth?'

False Verbs

One quite common type of error lies in wrongly treating as verbs words which are actually nouns, adjectives, or adverbs. Endings such as *-ed* are added, the auxiliaries *do* and *have* are put in front, and so on. 'False verbs' are the result.

251 Chance

Wrong: I wanted to see you, but I was not chanced.
Correct: I wanted to see you, but I didn't have the chance.

'Chance' is a verb in some contexts, a noun in others. As a verb it is followed by '*to* + verb', and means 'verb by chance', for example, 'chanced to see' means 'saw by chance'. 'Happen to' can be substituted for 'chance to':

> While on my way to the clinic, I chanced to see *or* happened to see a wallet lying on the ground.

'Chance' as a verb has no passive; 'am chanced', 'was chanced', etc. are not Standard English expressions.

252 Dead

Wrong: It was terrible to hear that he had dead.
Correct: It was terrible to hear that he had died. *or* that he was dead.

The parts of the regular verb 'die' are *die – died – died*. 'Dead' is an adjective meaning 'not alive'; it must follow some part of the verb 'be'.

253 Horn

Wrong: You must horn before overtaking.
Correct: You must sound your horn before overtaking.

'Horn' is a noun, not a verb.

254 Jealous

Wrong: She jealoused her sister because of her good fortune.

Correct: She was jealous of her sister because of her good fortune.

'Jealous' is an adjective, not a verb.

255 Less

Wrong: The radio seemed too expensive, and I asked him to less the price.

Correct: The radio seemed too expensive, and I asked him to reduce the price.

'Less' is an adjective, not a verb. There is a verb related to it, 'lessen'.

256 Naked

Wrong: He naked himself and entered the water.

Correct: He stripped off his clothes *or* He undressed and entered the water.

'Naked' is an adjective. It cannot be used as a verb, and there is no adverb form in *-ly*:

Wrong: He stripped off his clothes and went nakedly through the water.

Correct: He stripped off his clothes and went naked through the water.

257 Off

Wrong: Off the light!

Correct: Turn off the light! *or* Switch off the light!

'Off' is an adverb or a preposition, forming a phrasal or prepositional verb together with an ordinary verb; it cannot be a verb by itself. See page 113 for some remarks on phrasal verbs.

258 Opportune

Wrong: I wanted to see you, but I was not opportuned.

Correct: I wanted to see you, but I didn't have the
　　　　　opportunity.

Just as there is no verb 'be chanced', so there is no verb
'be opportuned'. In fact 'opportune' is not a verb at all;
it is an adjective meaning 'suitable':

　　　　　They will attack as soon as they consider circum-
　　　　　stances opportune.

259 Pregnant
Wrong: He denied that he was the one who pregnanted
　　　　　her. *or* who pregnated her.
Correct: He denied that he was the one who had made
　　　　　her pregnant.

'Pregnant' is an adjective not a verb, and there is no verb
'pregnate'. There is a verb 'impregnate', which means
'make pregnant', but it is used in biological discussion
rather than everyday discussion, and chiefly describes the
behaviour of non-human creatures.

260 Ready
Wrong: We can't leave yet, because Salihu doesn't
　　　　　ready.
Correct: We can't leave yet, because Salihu isn't ready.

'Ready' is an adjective, not a verb.

261 Senior
Wrong: The uncle of mine who has just died seniored
　　　　　my father.
Correct: The uncle of mine who has just died was
　　　　　senior to my father. *or* was my father's senior.
　　　　　or was my father's elder brother. *or* was older
　　　　　than my father.

'Senior' is an adjective (or an adjective functioning as a
noun), not a verb. 'Senior to' means 'older than'. Also to
be noted is 'the senior' (of the two), when two persons
are being compared in age:

Anne and Elizabeth are sisters; Anne is the senior (of the two).

262 Worth

Wrong: I bought that car for ₦6000, but now I'd say it didn't worth it.

Correct: I bought that car for ₦6000, but now I'd say it wasn't worth it.

Wrong: He doesn't worth the trouble one takes over him.

Correct: He isn't worth the trouble one takes over him.

'Worth' is an adjective, not a verb. See also pages 213–4 and 230–31.

Now do Exercises 18 to 30.

7 Prepositions

Prepositions are another class of small and important words which can be found in almost any English sentence; *in, at, on, with, by, from, of, to, for, into*, etc. These are one-word or *simple* prepositions; there are also *complex* prepositions made up of more than one word: *up to, as for, because of, owing to*, etc. A preposition must be followed by a noun phrase. (See pages 195–6.) Preposition + noun phrase form a prepositional phrase.

The chief difficulty for the learner is to decide which preposition to use before which noun, or noun phrase. The most frequent errors arise from the over-use of *at* and *on*, though these, together with *in*, are the most common prepositions in English in any case. Errors in the use of prepositions may not cause misunderstanding, but as in other areas of grammar they give an appearance of imperfect or careless learning which the more ambitious student will want to remedy.

A list of common prepositional phrases is found on pages 227–30.

'At' wrongly used

263 Age

Wrong: He started writing books at his old age.
Correct: He started writing books in his old age.

Wrong: Man did not use metals at the Stone Age.
Correct: Man did not use metals in the Stone Age.

'Age' here means a *period* of time, so 'in' is the right preposition. 'At' is correct when 'age' means a point in time, for example:

You should no longer be working so hard at your age.

264 Large cities, countries, etc.
Wrong: My brother Usman is now living at London.
Correct: My brother Usman is now living in London.

Wrong: My sister spent her long vacation at America.
or at Nigeria. *or* at Rivers State.
Correct: My sister spent her long vacation in America.
or in Nigeria. *or* in Rivers State.

'In' should be used before names of cities, countries, and parts of countries (states, provinces, etc.). 'At' is used before names of small towns, villages, etc.

265 Arrival
Wrong: At my arrival, they referred me to the Security Officer.
Correct: On my arrival, they referred me to the Security Officer.

266 Middle
Wrong: He stopped at the middle of the paragraph.
Correct: He stopped in the middle of the paragraph.

Wrong: He stood at the middle of the room.
Correct: He stood in the middle of the room.

267 Alert
Wrong: We must be at the alert; lions are in the neighbourhood.
Correct: We must be on the alert; lions are in the neighbourhood.

268 Scene
Wrong: She is a well-known figure at the international scene.
Correct: She is a well-known figure on the international scene.

In contrast to 'on the international scene' there is 'at the international level'.

269 Back

Wrong: Look in your mirror; there's a lorry coming at your back.

Correct: Look in your mirror; there's a lorry coming behind you.

Wrong: I hate people talking about me at my back.

Correct: I hate people talking about me behind my back.

The back of something is still part of that thing; so, while the use of 'at the back' is wrong in the above examples, we can say:

> He sat at the back of the room.
> At the back of his mind was always the fear of failure.

270 Front

Wrong: A huge bus was at my front, slowing us all down.

Correct: A huge bus was in front of me, slowing us all down.

This example is similar to the last one. 'At the front of' can be used to mean 'in the front part of . . .', for example:

> He sat at the front of the class.

'On' wrongly used

271 Table

Wrong: They were on the table when I entered, and told me to come and join the meal.

Correct: They were at table when I entered, and told me to come and join the meal.

272 Expense

Wrong: You will make the journey on my expense.

Correct: You will make the journey at my expense.

Do not confuse 'at my expense' with 'on my account', which often means 'for my sake':

> Do not make the journey just on my account; you can write to me.

273 Battlefront
Wrong: The guerilla leader died on the battlefront.
Correct: The guerilla leader died at the battlefront.

But say 'on the battlefield', for example:

> The issue will be decided on the battlefield.

274 Speed
Wrong: Mr Johnson drove on top speed to the hospital.
Correct: Mr Johnson drove at top speed to the hospital.

275 Gear
Wrong: He drove the remaining thirty kilometres on second gear.
Correct: He drove the remaining thirty kilometres in second gear.

276 Bed
Wrong: Jacob was already on bed when I called.
Correct: Jacob was already in bed when I called.

'In bed' is the correct expression even when someone is lying on top of any sheets or blankets, rather than inside or underneath them. But 'on' is correct if a determiner comes before 'bed', and the person is not under the sheets or blankets:

> Jacob was sitting on his bed reading a book.

277 The Long Run
Wrong: On the long run you will find that buying cheap clothes is a false economy.
Correct: In the long run you will find that buying cheap clothes is a false economy.

278 Exile

Wrong: The deposed President went on exile.
Correct: The deposed President went into exile.

Wrong: The leader of the Farmers' Party is now on exile.
Correct: The leader of the Farmers' Party is now in exile.

279 Face

Wrong: He accused me of embezzlement; he said it on my face.
Correct: He accused me of embezzlement; he said it to my face.

'To my face' is an idiom meaning 'to me as he faced me'; 'on my face' can be used with literal meaning:

> There were many pimples on my face.

280 Line

Wrong: The cooks refused to serve Festus because he had not been waiting on the line.
Correct: The cooks refused to serve Festus because he had not been waiting in the line.

The meaning is that Festus had not joined the line so as to await his turn for food. 'On the line' has the meaning 'touching the line', not above it or below it, for example:

> Your work always looks so untidy – it seems you just can't write on the line.

281 Time

Wrong: His driving will improve on time.
Correct: His driving will improve in time. *or* will improve eventually.

'In time' but not 'on time' can mean 'eventually'.

Wrong: If you don't repair that roof on time your house will get flooded when the rains start.

| *Correct:* | If you don't repair that roof in time your house will get flooded when the rains start. |

'On time' means 'at exactly the right time'. 'In time' means not 'at any fixed time', but 'early enough'. 'On time' could be used like this:

> That lecturer never arrives on time. He's usually at least ten minutes late, though once he came ten minutes too early.

282 Way

| *Wrong:* | I could not enter the left-hand lane because there was a bus on my way. |
| *Correct:* | I could not enter the left-hand lane because there was a bus in my way. |

'In my way' is the correct expression meaning 'blocking the way'. 'On my way' means 'While going'. Also see number 317.

'With' wrongly used
283 Train, bus, car, etc.

| *Wrong:* | Mr Gatuma went from Nairobi to Mombasa with train. |
| *Correct:* | Mr Gatuma went from Nairobi to Mombasa by train. |

| *Wrong:* | The Party Chairman arrived at the rally with helicopter. |
| *Correct:* | The Party Chairman arrived at the rally by helicopter. |

284 Leg

| *Wrong:* | Ikenna went to the campus with leg. |
| *Correct:* | Ikenna went to the campus on foot. |

It is also wrong to say 'Ikenna used leg to go to the campus'.

285 Names of languages

| *Wrong:* | I spoke to him with English, but he answered me with Yoruba. *or* with Swahili. |

Correct: I spoke to him in English, but he answered me in Yoruba. *or* in Swahili.

286 Belief, hope, etc.
Wrong: I have come to you with the belief that you are an expert.
Correct: I have come to you in the belief that you are an expert.

Wrong: He went to Gaborone with the hope of obtaining redress.
Correct: He went to Gaborone in the hope of obtaining redress.

See also number 54.

287 Danger
Wrong: Kwesi is with danger of not even getting a pass mark.
Correct: Kwesi is in danger of not even getting a pass mark.

288 Wrongly used after **charge**
Wrong: Yinka was in charge with all the catering arrangements.
Correct: Yinka was in charge of all the catering arrangements.

In this example 'charge' is a noun. It can also be used as a verb, and then it can be followed by 'with', for example:

> They charged her with the task of looking after their guests.
> He was charged with assaulting a police officer.

'To' wrongly used

289 Opinion
Wrong: To my opinion, no mercy should be shown to armed robbers.
Correct: In my opinion, no mercy should be shown to armed robbers.

290 Regard, respect

Wrong: Olu was very good at mathematics. To this regard *or* To this respect, he was different from his brothers.

Correct: Olu was very good at mathematics. In this regard *or* In this respect, he was different from his brothers.

It is never correct to say 'To this regard', 'To this respect'. Sometimes we can say 'With respect to', 'With regard to' something, for example:

With respect to eating habits, the pig is herbivorous.

291 Practice

Wrong: Now he has to put to practice what he has learned.

Correct: Now he has to put into practice what he has learned.

Here 'into' and not 'to' is correct; but also note some examples where 'to' and not 'into' is correct:

Wrong: They came into an agreement *or* They came into a compromise over the boundary question.

Correct: They came to an agreement *or* They came to a compromise over the boundary question.

292 Existence

Wrong: The United Nations Organization came to existence in 1945.

Correct: The United Nations Organization came into existence in 1945.

293 To wrongly used after accordance

Wrong: In accordance to Government regulations, your annual leave is forfeited.

Correct: In accordance with Government regulations, your annual leave is forfeited.

Other Prepositions wrongly used

294 Among

Wrong: They flocked to the stadium, but I was not among. *or* I was not among of them.

Correct: They flocked to the stadium, but I was not among them.

'Among' is a preposition requiring a noun or pronoun after it. 'Among of' is not Standard English.

295 As and like

Wrong: He talks as a businessman, though he isn't one.

Correct: He talks like a businessman, though he isn't one.

The same meaning could be given by a clause beginning with 'as'; or, better, with 'as if':

>He talks as if he were a businessman, though he isn't one.

In the following examples, 'as' is correct:

>She appeared as Lady Macbeth.
>He dressed as a Leopard Chief.

The idea here is that an actor fully enters into the character being impersonated, and does not just act 'like' that character.

296 As wrongly followed by to

Wrong: The pigs are to be slaughtered today. As to the chickens, they should be sold off.

Correct: The pigs are to be slaughtered today. As for the chickens, they should be sold off.

'As for' is the right prepositional phrase to use when introducing a new topic of conversation in the manner of the example. Using 'as for' often indicates that the speaker has just thought of something which should not be left out.

297 **Before** wrongly used

Wrong: Applicants should bring their testimonials before one month.

Correct: Applicants should bring their testimonials within one month. *or* before one month is over.

'Within' here is used to mean 'at any time from now but not later than' one month.

298 **By** wrongly used with clock time

Wrong: I told Chima to come by 3 o'clock; I was surprised to see him at 2.45.

Correct: I told Chima to come at 3 o'clock; I was surprised to see him at 2.45.

'By' when used with a stated time does not mean 'at' or 'on the stroke of'; it means 'any time up to and including, but not later than . . .' In the wrong example, if Chima came by – that is, before – 3 o'clock, there was no cause for surprise.

Misundestanding can clearly result from this misuse of 'by'.

299 **By** wrongly used with **then**

Wrong: I got married in 1960. My brother was struggling to become a soccer star by then.

Correct: I got married in 1960. My brother was struggling to become a soccer star then. *or* at that time.

'By then' really means 'before then', and is found with perfect tenses.

'Then' has two meanings: (1) 'at that time',; (2) 'after that'. When it means 'after that' it can be put at the beginning of the sentence, but not when it means 'at that time':

> He flung the net out over the water. Then he sat down calmly to wait.

300 By wrongly used with names of places

Wrong: Mr Mingi went to Karachi by Rome.
Correct: Mr Mingi went to Karachi via Rome.

'Via' is the word used in the context of travelling to mean 'passing through'.

301 Into wrongly used before **touch, contact**

Wrong: I will have to get into touch with a lawyer.
Correct: I will have to get in touch with a lawyer.

Wrong: Get into contact with the Chief Engineer, and he'll help you.
Correct: Get in contact with the Chief Engineer, and he'll help you.

302 Since

Wrong: Adekunle came to live in Ibadan since 1972.
Correct: Adekunle came to live in Ibadan in 1972.

'Since' cannot be used after the Past Simple Tense. It can be used after perfect tenses, and means from such-and-such a time onwards'.

Adekunle has been living in Ibadan since 1972.

303 Under

Wrong: She was under pregnancy, and could not lift anything heavy.
Correct: She was pregnant, and could not lift anything heavy.

'Under' can be used in many expressions; under contract, under control, under supervision, under consideration, under repair; but 'under pregnancy' is not standard English.

304 Unless

Wrong: Nobody knows anything about photography, unless Andrew.
Correct: Nobody knows anything about photography, except Andrew.

Another way of expressing the meaning of the sentence is by using 'only':

> Only Andrew knows anything about photography.

305 Until

Wrong: Read until Chapter 20; you can leave the rest.
Correct: Read as far as Chapter 20 *or* Read down to Chapter 20; you can leave the rest.

'Until' is a preposition of time.

306 Until and on wrongly used together

Wrong: Do not pay him until on Wednesday.
Correct: Do not pay him until Wednesday.

'On' is the right preposition to use before names of days of the week, but it is not used with 'until'.

307 Upon wrongly used

Wrong: Upon all our efforts to help him, he preferred his life of crime.
Correct: In spite of all our efforts to help him, he preferred his life of crime.

Now do Exercises 31 to 34.

8 Adverbials

Adverbials include one-word adverbs (e.g. *now, there, away, slowly*), prepositional phrases (*on Tuesday, at home, to the farm,* etc.); clauses (*before you arrive, if he comes,* etc.); noun phrases (*last week, last year,* etc.), and other types. They can be classified into adverbials of *time, place, manner, degree,* etc. They usually 'modify' a verb, but some adverbials can play other modifying roles. Altogether adverbials are a very mixed group.

Common errors treated here include the misuse of adverbs of time and degree, and the wrong positioning of adverbs. Another quite common error is to give the wrong meaning to an adverbial clause through the wrong choice of conjunction: see the subsection 'Clauses Wrongly Conjoined'. A few examples of adverbs confused because of similar meaning are found in Chapter 11.

Manner Adverbs

A very large number of adverbs, including most adverbs of manner, are formed by adding *-ly* to an adjective: *slow* (adjective), *slowly* (adverb); *secret, secretly,* etc. This is not possible if the adjective already ends in *-ly,* e.g. *likely.* There are also a few other adjectives which do not add *-ly* to form an adverb, for example:

308 Fast
> *Wrong:* She ran fastly because the train was coming.
> *Correct:* She ran fast because the train was coming.

Time Adverbs

309 After wrongly used
> *Wrong:* The doctor is busy at present. Come again after.

Correct: The doctor is busy at present. Come again later.

'After' should not be used by itself as an adverb of time.

310 As of now
Wrong: As at now Musa is trying to build a house.
Correct: As of now Musa is trying to build a house.

311 Before wrongly used
Wrong: I last visited the zoo before three years. *or* three years before.
Correct: I last visited the zoo three years ago.

When used as a preposition of time, 'before' means 'earlier than . . .':

> There were powerful states in Africa before the coming of the Europeans.

'Before' can also be used as an adverb, usually coming at the end of a clause or a sentence, and meaning 'earlier than this':

> I have never set eyes on him before.

But 'ago' is the right word meaning 'at such-and-such a point in time before the present'.

312 Ever wrongly used
Wrong: He has ever believed that he would succeed.

Correct: He has always believed that he would succeed.

'Ever' cannot be used just like 'always' to mean 'at all times', although it does have this meaning in the prayer formula 'for ever and ever'.
 'Ever' is usually found in questions and negative sentences, and means 'at any time', for example:

> Did he ever tell you about his hobbies?

313 For some time
Wrong: Ifeanyi has been avoiding him for some times.

Correct: Ifeanyi has been avoiding him for some time.

'For some time' means 'over quite a long period', and is an adverbial phrase indicating *duration*. There is no phrase 'for some times'. There is, however, an adverb 'sometimes', meaning 'occasionally':

> Bola sometimes gets impatient, but on the whole remains very even-tempered.

314 **Not long** wrongly used
Wrong: Her labour pains began. Not quite long, she gave birth to a male child.
Correct: Her labour pains began. Soon afterwards, *or* Not long afterwards, she gave birth to a male child.

'Not (quite) long' is not a standard English adverbial; 'not long' can be used like this:

> It was not long before she gave birth to a male child.

315 **Recently**
Wrong: I haven't talked to Veronica of recent.
Correct: I haven't talked to Veronica recently. *or* of late.

'Of recent' used with no noun following is not Standard English.

316 **Since** wrongly used
Wrong: So you didn't see Bayo? But he has been here since.
Correct: So you didn't see Bayo? But he has been here for a long time.

'Since' cannot be used to mean 'for a long time'; it cannot stand alone as an adverb of time.

317 **(While) on my way** wrongly used
Wrong: On my way going *or* While on my way going I saw a python cross the road.

Correct: While on my way *or* While going I saw a
python cross the road.

Do not join 'on my way' and 'going' in one phrase. 'While
going' is a short and quite correct form of 'while I was
going'. We can likewise say 'while sleeping', 'while
eating', and so on.

Adverbs of Degree

318 **Extremely** and **very** wrongly used together

Wrong: I was extremely very happy to hear of your
victory.

Correct: I was extremely *or* very *or* very, very happy to
hear of your victory.

'Extremely' and 'very' cannot be used together. 'Very,
very' is not wrong, but in general it is advisable not to
stress words by repeating them.

319 **Quite** wrongly used instead of **very**

Wrong: The water was quite hot, so I badly scalded
myself.

Correct: The was very hot, so I badly scalded myself.

Wrong: Paul drove quite fast, with the result that he
overtook every vehicle on the road.

Correct: Paul drove very fast, with the result that he
overtook every vehicle on the road.

'Quite' sometimes means 'very' or 'completely', but with
adjectives or adverbs in common use that can be thought
of as a scale it often means 'somewhat', 'moderately', for
example, 'quite hot', 'quite fast'. So in the first example,
if the water was only *quite* hot I would not have scalded
myself; in the second, if Paul drove only quite fast, he
probably would not have overtaken every other vehicle.

Examples of correct use of 'quite' meaning 'moderately':

The water was quite hot – hot enough for a bath,
anyway.

> Paul drove quite fast, but it still took him many hours to reach Kano.

Also see number 576.

320 Unnecessary use of **quite**

Wrong: His work wasn't all that quite impressive.
Correct: His work wasn't all that impressive.

Wrong: His experience of life overseas wasn't all that quite happy.
Correct: His experience of life overseas wasn't all that happy.

'Not all that' must come immediately before an adjective or adverb; it cannot be followed by articles or other adverbs of degree.

321 **So much** wrongly used

Wrong: Metu is so much sad that he has vowed to kill himself.
Correct: Metu is so sad that he has vowed to kill himself.

'So much' and 'so' are like 'too much' and 'too' in that 'so much' cannot be used before adverbs and adjectives. 'So much' is used after verbs, and is followed by 'that', for example:

> It has rained so much recently that all the roads must be impassable.

322 **Somehow** wrongly used

Wrong: Jegede is somehow careless: he has lost his key again.
Correct: Jegede is somewhat careless *or* rather careless: he has lost his key again.

'Somehow' means 'in some way or other', not 'to some extent', and cannot be used as an adverb of degree before adjectives and adverbs. It can be used at the beginning of a sentence or before a verb, for example:

Somehow he managed to get the door open again.

323 **Too** wrongly used instead of **too much**

Wrong: Uche too likes dancing.
Correct: Uche likes dancing too much. *or* Uche is too fond of dancing.

'Too' can only be used before adjectives and adverbs, not before verbs. 'Too much' is used after verbs.

324 **Too** wrongly used instead of **so**

Wrong: His words were too insulting that they reported him to the Oba.
Correct: His words were so insulting that they reported him to the Oba.

'So' here means 'to such an extent'. 'Too' cannot be followed by 'that'.

325 **Too** wrongly used instead of **very**

Wrong: She said she loved watching that TV programme; it was too funny.
Correct: She said she loved watching that TV programme; it was very funny.

'Too' before adjectives and adverbs means 'beyond the limit', 'beyond what is acceptable'; use of 'too' often therefore indicates disapproval:

He spoke too softly – no one could hear him.
He spoke too softly for anyone to hear him.

Miscellaneous Adverbs

326 **Again** wrongly used (1)

Wrong: Here are the matches. What do you need again?
Correct: Here are the matches. What else do you need?

Wrong: You must have liked California. Where did you go again?

Correct: You must have liked California. Where else did you go?

Wrong: Let me write down your names: Eunice, Mary, . . . Who again?

Correct: Let me write down your names: Eunice, Mary, . . . Who else?

327 **Again** wrongly used (2)

Wrong: I still have far to go, and I have no money again.

Correct: I still have far to go, and I have no more money. *or* no money left.

Wrong: I have answered all your questions, and have nothing to say again.

Correct: I have answered all your questions, and have nothing more to say.

Wrong: All my savings are exhausted, and I have nothing again.

Correct: All my savings are exhausted, and I have nothing left.

328 **Also** wrongly used

Wrong: Ali had no money, and Yakubu hadn't any also.

Correct: Ali had no money, and Yakubu hadn't any either.

Wrong: My wife doesn't eat butter, and I don't eat it also.

Correct: My wife doesn't eat butter, and I don't eat it either.

'Either', not 'also', is required after the preceding 'not' of 'don't'.

329 **Anyway** wrongly used

Wrong: A: What were your results like? B: Anyway, I had one Credit.

Correct: A: What were your results like? B: Well, I had one Credit.

Speaker 'B' appears to be on the defensive; 'well' would help to cover up his hesitation.

'Anyway' means 'whatever happens', 'whatever the case may be'; it softens or modifies some unpleasant-sounding remark that has gone before, for example:

> The film's been cancelled. But I didn't really want to go anyway.

330 **Never** wrongly used
Wrong: Dickson is never a sportsman, in spite of his interest in games.
Correct: Dickson is no sportsman, in spite of his interest in games.

Wrong: He is never a speaker, though he reads a lot.
Correct: He is no speaker, though he reads a lot.

331 **Not at all**
Example A: Do you approve of loans for farmers?
Wrong: B: At all.
Correct: B: Not at all.

'At all' should always be used after a negative word.

332 **Yes, please; No, thank you**
Example A: Will you have something to eat?
Wrong: B: No, please.
Correct: B: No, thank you.

'Please' cannot follow 'No'; it can only follow 'Yes'.

333 **Yes** and **no** after negative questions
Example A: You aren't the owner of this machine, are you?
Wrong: B: Yes, it belongs to one of my friends.
Correct: B: No, it belongs to one of my friends.

It is 'No' here which means 'You are right', 'What you have said is true'.

Adverbs misplaced

Many errors are caused by inability to decide correctly which position an adverbial should occupy in a sentence. The learner's task is made more difficult by the fact that, while the position of some adverbials cannot be varied – see number 337, for example – most of them can occupy more than one position. That still does not mean that an adverbial can just be inserted at random in a sentence. There are three main permitted positions:

1 FRONT POSITION:	*On Tuesday* they held a meeting.
2 MID-POSITION:	They *often* hold meetings.
	They have *just* held a meeting.
	They have *just* been holding a meeting.
3 END POSITION:	They held a meeting *on Tuesday*.

But, again, though these are the permitted positions, not every adverbial can occupy all three positions. One fairly reliable rule is that adverbial phrases and clauses cannot occupy mid-position, whereas some one-word adverbs can be found in all three positions. It is one-word adverbs, in fact, which cause the most difficulty. Making the right choice ultimately depends on knowing which *type* of adverb is being used (time, place, manner, etc.), and on knowing the rules governing the placement of that type.

Note finally here that 'mid-position' has three varieties: (i) between the subject and the verb; (ii) after the auxiliary, if an auxiliary comes before the verb; (iii) after the first auxiliary, if two auxiliaries come before the verb. 'Mid-position' *cannot* mean between the verb and its object. Putting it there is a common error, as numbers 334 to 336 illustrate.

334 Quickly

Wrong: He pushed quickly his bicycle out of the way.
Correct: 1 He quickly pushed his bicycle out of the way.

2 He pushed his bicycle quickly out of the way.

3 He pushed his bicycle out of the way quickly.

4 Quickly he pushed his bicycle out of the way.

Of the correct sentences, (1) and (3) are more likely than (2) and (4). Putting an adverb of manner in front position, as in (4), gives emphasis to it.

335 Now

Wrong: He is copying now those exercises.

Correct: 1 Now he is copying those exercises.

2 He is now copying those exercises.

3 He is copying those exercises now.

This is an adverb of time which can occupy all three positions, though front position, as in (1), would be chosen for emphasis. Other adverbs of time which behave in the same way are 'recently', 'often', 'sometimes', 'once', 'then', 'again', 'already', 'still'.

336 Always

Wrong: 1 He asks me always very difficult questions.

2 Always he asks me very difficult questions.

Correct: He always asks me very difficult questions.

'Always' takes mid-position. So also do 'ever', 'never', 'seldom', 'hardly', and 'hardly ever'. The last four of these can also take front position – but see number 206.

337 Before

Wrong: I have before seen many masquerades.

Correct: I have seen many masquerades before.

'Before' as an adverb of time should always occupy end position.

338 Enough

Wrong: This knife is not enough sharp.

Correct: This knife is not sharp enough.

'Enough' comes *after* adjectives and adverbs, but *before* nouns.

339 Even

Wrong: Eze insulted his father. Even, he said he would never come home again.

Correct: Eze insulted his father. He even said he would never come home again.

'Even' usually emphasizes the word that comes after it. In the above example 'even' ought to emphasize the verb 'said', not the subject 'he'. When it does emphasize the subject, 'even' is the first word in the sentence, but then it must not be followed by a comma:

Wrong: They all opposed their father. Even, Ada was against him.

Correct: They all opposed their father. Even Ada was against him.

340 Not misplaced

Wrong: All men do not wish to live to a great age.
Correct: Not all men wish to live to a great age.

'Not' usually occupies mid-position, but here it must precede 'all' to show that the wish to live to a great age is not shared by everybody. The wrong sentence is grammatically correct, but it does not give the meaning we should expect.

Clauses wrongly joined

Adverbial clauses are joined to main clauses by means of CONJUNCTIONS, each giving a particular meaning to the clause and to the sentence as a whole: *if, unless, provided* (condition); *when, after, before, as soon as* (time); *as, since, because* (reason); *although, though* (concession or contrast), etc. Certain errors arise through the misuse of conjunctions, and some can cause misunderstanding. Also see pages 192–5.

341 Hence wrongly used

Wrong: Rotimi decided to sell the land, hence the
price of cocoa had fallen very low.

Correct: 1 Rotimi decided to sell the land, since the
price of cocoa had fallen very low.

2 The price of cocoa had fallen very low;
hence Rotimi decided to sell the land.

'Hence' means 'as a result', 'therefore', 'for this reason';
it does not mean 'because' or 'since'. Note that 'since' can
be either an adverb of time, or a conjunction introducing
a clause of reason.

342 For the fact that and being that wrongly used

Wrong: For the fact that you belong to a low-income
group, your difficulties are appreciated.

Correct: Since you belong to a low-income group, your
difficulties are appreciated.

'For the fact that' should not be used to introduce a
clause of reason, and is generally a clumsy phrase.
'Since' is the best word to use.

There is a phrase 'but for the fact that', used to introduce a clause of negative condition:

But for the fact that we are a peace-loving
nation, we might have gone to war with you.

This could be just as well expressed thus:

If we were not a peace-loving nation, we might
have gone to war with you.

'Being that' is another wrong way of introducing a clause
of reason; 'since' is again the best word to use. 'Being
that' could however be found following a noun.

He left the meeting in a hurry, his excuse being
that he had to take his wife to hospital.

343 If and to say wrongly used together

Wrong: If to say you had been here earlier, you would
easily have succeeded.

> *Correct:* If you had been here earlier, you would easily
> have succeeded.

'To say' must never be inserted after 'if'; it can sometimes
be used after 'as if', introducing a clause of manner:

> He was staring in all directions, as if to say he
> had never been here before.

344 **Should** wrongly followed by **in case**
Wrong: Should in case you see him, please tell him to
come quickly. •
Correct: 1 Should you see him, please tell him to come
quickly.
2 If you (should) see him, please tell him to
come quickly.

'In case' essentially means 'for fear that':

> Wind your windows up in case it rains.

345 Wrong use of **had it been**
Wrong: Had it been (that) you informed me earlier, I
would have included your name.
Correct: Had you informed me *or* If you had informed
me earlier, I would have included your name.

Do not use 'Had it been (that) . . .' in a conditional clause
where there is another verb in the clause ('informed' in
the above example'). 'Had it been' can sometimes be used
where there is no other verb in the clause, for example:

> Had it been me *or* If I had been you I would not
> have allowed them to spend even one night in
> my house.

346 **So far as** wrongly used
Wrong: So far as you are a student, you will pay only
half fare.
Correct: Provided you are a student *or* Since you are a
student, you will pay only half fare.

'Provided' means 'if and only if', 'on condition that';

111

'since' here means 'because'. Either 'provided' or 'since' would give meaning to the sentence. The meaning of 'so far as' is 'to the extent that', 'up to the point that', for example:

> So far as I know, Nnamdi has settled all his outstanding debts.

347 **Except** wrongly used

Wrong: Except you press this knob, you will not be able to take any pictures.

Correct: Unless you press this knob, you will not be able to take any pictures.

'Except' cannot be used as a conjunction introducing a conditional clause in modern English. For the confusion of 'unless' and 'except', also see number 304.

348 **Yet** wrongly used after **although, though**

Wrong: Though the wall was high, *or* Although the wall was high, yet the prisoner managed to escape.

Correct: Though the wall was high, *or* Although the wall was high, the prisoner managed to escape.

When contrasting two points, do not follow 'although' with 'yet'. Conversely, do not precede 'yet' with 'although'. This usage was at one time possible, but nowadays sounds archaic.

Now do exercises 35 to 39.

9 Phrasal and Prepositional Verbs

Phrasal and prepositional verbs differ from ordinary verbs in that the dictionary form consists of more than one word. A PHRASAL VERB (e.g., *take up, look after, fall through*) consists of an ordinary verb plus one of a small group of adverbs (*in, out, off, over, across, after, back, through, up, down*, etc.). A PREPOSITIONAL VERB (e.g., *believe in, rely on, apply for*) consists of an ordinary verb plus a preposition (*on, of, for, to, with, at*, etc.). It is sometimes difficult to distinguish between the two because some words – 'in', for example – function both as adverbs and prepositions. There are many similarities between the two groups, which is why they are treated together here.

The errors in this area mostly occur when a verb is followed by an adverb or a preposition when it should not be; alternatively when it is not followed by an adverb or preposition, but ought to be; and when the wrong adverb or preposition is used.

To avoid errors the verb and the adverb or preposition need to be learned together.

In what follows, all errors concerning phrasal verbs are first treated. Then prepositional verbs are treated according to the type of error made.

Phrasal Verbs

An added difficulty with phrasal verbs is that in some cases the object of the verb can come between the verb and the adverb, and must come between the verb and the adverb if it is a personal pronoun object: *He switched the light on; He switched on the light: He switched it on*. The phrasal verb is here said to be SEPARABLE. Some phrasal verbs, however, are INSEPARABLE – the verb and the adverb cannot be separated.

349 Throw away

Wrong: I gave him the letter, but he threw away it.
Correct: I gave him the letter, but he threw it away.

The phrasal verb 'throw away' is separable.

350 **Back** wrongly used after **return, recover**

Wrong: Arinze went to Kaduna yesterday, but he returned back this morning.
Correct: Arinze went to Kaduna yesterday, but he returned this morning *or* came back this morning.

'Return' means 'come back', so 'back' is redundant.

Wrong: Okafor had invested a lot of money, but he recovered none of it back.
Correct: Okafor had invested a lot of money but he recovered none of it, *or* he got none of it back.

'Recover' in this example means 'get back', so 'back' is redundant.

351 **Up** wrongly used after **cope**

Wrong: He was unable to cope up with so many demands.
Correct: He was unable to cope with so many demands.

'Cope' is not followed by 'up'.

352 **Up** wrongly used after **wash**

Wrong: He was covered with cement and went to wash up.
Correct: He was covered with cement and went to wash *or* to have a wash.

'Wash up' is never used for washing the body. It is used for the washing of plates, etc, after a meal:
   She likes to wash up immediately after eating.

353 **Out** wrongly used after **voice**

Wrong: He didn't want to voice out his opinion.
Correct: He didn't want to voice his opinion.

354 **Up** wrongly omitted after **pick**

Wrong: Mr Udoh came at four o'clock to pick me.
Correct: Mr Udoh came at four o'clock to pick me up.

There is an ordinary verb 'pick' and a phrasal verb 'pick up'; 'pick up' is needed here, meaning 'collect in his car'.

355 **Out** wrongly omitted after **turn**

Wrong: We thought he was a Kenyan, but he turned to be a Tanzanian.
Correct: We thought he was a Kenyan, but he turned out to be a Tanzanian.

'He turned out to be' means 'His correct identity was revealed as . . .'; 'turn to' means 'adopt as a different course of action', for example:

> He was once so careful with his money that everyone was surprised when he turned to a life of extravagance.

356 **Up** wrongly omitted after **draw**

Wrong: They met to draw a new constitution.
Correct: They met to draw up a new constitution.

'Draw up' means 'compose' when referring to written documents. 'Draw' without 'up' means 'compose' in the sense of 'make a picture':

> I sat still while he drew my portrait.

357 **Care for** and **care about** confused

Wrong: He drives so recklessly, it seems he doesn't care for his life.
Correct: He drives so recklessly, it seems he doesn't care about his life.

'Care about' something means 'consider something as having value'. 'Care for' someone means 'devote time and sympathy' to someone:

> She sees it as her duty to care for her aged parents.

Sometimes 'care for' can mean 'like':

> I don't much care for sugary food.

Verbs wrongly used without a Preposition

358 Approve

Wrong: I do not approve your associating with that boy.

Correct: I do not approve of your associating with that boy.

In this example 'approve' means 'like', 'think good'; it must be followed by 'of'. 'Approve' without 'of' means 'give formal sanction to', as in this example:

> He did not approve the students' claim for a feeding allowance.

359 Communicate

Wrong: Please communicate me as soon as your result comes through.

Correct: Please inform me *or* Please get in touch with me as soon as your result comes through.

In this example 'communicate' clearly means 'inform' or 'contact in order to inform'. 'Communicate', not followed by 'with', cannot be used in this sense. When 'communicate' does mean 'inform' it is followed by 'something *to* somebody', for example:

> He communicated the news of his result to me.

'Communicate with' often means 'have dealings with':

> He lives alone, and hardly communicates with anyone.

360 Discriminate

Wrong: It is unethical to discriminate one's fellow human beings.

Correct: It is unethical to discriminate against one's fellow human beings.

'Discriminate' must be followed by 'against' before the victim of the discrimination is mentioned. Sometimes it can be used intransitively:

> He treats everyone alike; he doesn't discriminate.

361 Dispose

Wrong: You should dispose your radio, and get a new one.

Correct: You should dispose of your radio, and get a new one.

'Dispose' meaning 'do away with' is followed by 'of'.

362 Insist

Wrong: He insisted to see the Permanent Secretary.

Correct: He insisted on seeing the Permanent Secretary.

363 Operate

Wrong: The doctor decided to operate him immediately.

Correct: The doctor decided to operate on him immediately.

Wrong: He was operated for appendicitis.

Correct: He was operated on for appendicitis.

364 Preside

Wrong: Mr Olu was asked to preside the meeting.

Correct: Mr Olu was asked to preside over the meeting.

365 Reply

Wrong: You should reply his letter immediately.

Correct: You should reply to his letter immediately.

366 Search

Wrong: He searched my file everywhere, but couldn't find it.

Correct: He searched for my file everywhere, but couldn't find it.

'Search' is followed immediately by a direct object when the direct object refers to the person or to the place where something is expected to be found:

> The policemen searched us thoroughly, but found nothing.

When 'search' means 'look for', it must be followed by 'for'.

367 Side

Wrong: Daniel always sides his son in the children's quarrels.

Correct: Daniel always sides with his son *or* always takes his son's side in the children's quarrels.

Wrong: Why do you always side him? Do you think he is always right?

Correct: Why do you always side with him? *or* always take his side? Do you think he is always right?

368 Succeed

Wrong: The poor woman succeeded to find her lost child.

Correct: The poor woman succeeded in finding her lost child.

369 Tamper

Wrong: Someone had been tampering the locks.

Correct: Someone had been tampering with the locks.

370 Think

Wrong: I am sure you are happy here, and never think to move.

Correct: I am sure you are happy here, and never think of moving.

'Think of', followed by a noun (including verb-nouns ending in *-ing*) means 'consider', as in the above example.

'Think to' followed by an infinitive is less common, and means 'remember to':

> His room is a complete mess, but he never thinks to tidy it.

Verbs wrongly used with a Preposition

371 Advocate
> *Wrong:* They advocated for the abolition of the death penalty.
>
> *Correct:* They advocated the abolition of the death penalty.

372 Answer
> *Wrong:* You should answer to his letter immediately.
>
> *Correct:* You should answer his letter immediately.

Also see number 365. In these examples 'answer' and 'reply' are verbs. But they can also function as nouns and then 'to' will be required after each:

> Please send your answers to this address. Do not make any reply to any of his questions.

373 Claim
> *Wrong:* They are only claiming for what is due to them.
>
> *Correct:* They are only claiming what is due to them.

'Claim' as a verb is not followed by 'for'; 'for' is used after 'claim' when it is a noun:

> He put in a claim for the refund of his expenses.

374 Comprise and consist of
> *Wrong:* The departmental block comprises of four lecture rooms.
>
> *Correct:* The departmental block comprises *or* consists of *or* is comprised of four lecture rooms.

'Comprise' can be used in the active or in the passive; only in the passive is it followed by 'of'. 'Consist' is used only in the active, and is followed by 'of'.

375 Demand
> *Wrong:* They are demanding for their annual increment.
>
> *Correct:* They are demanding their annual increment.

In this example 'demand' is a verb, and 'for' must not be used. Only when 'demand' is a noun can it be followed by 'for':

> They rejected his demand for compassionate leave.

376 Discuss

Wrong: They discussed about the proposal to withdraw from the talks.

Correct: They discussed the proposal to withdraw from the talks.

377 Doubt

Wrong: I doubt of his story; it sounds incredible.

Correct: I doubt *or* I have doubts about his story; it sounds incredible.

Wrong: I doubt of whether he deserves so much praise.

Correct: I doubt whether he deserves so much praise.

Wrong: He doubts of his ability to score three goals this time.

Correct: He doubts *or* He has doubts about his ability to score three goals this time.

'Doubt' in these examples is a verb, and normally it must not be followed by 'of'. Where 'doubt' as a verb means 'question the truth of' or 'lack confidence in', 'have doubts about' can be used instead. 'Of' is commonly found in the phrase 'in doubt of', where 'doubt' is a noun:

> They were in no doubt of eventual victory.

378 Enter

Wrong: He entered into the already crowded room.

Correct: He entered the already crowded room.

When 'enter' means 'physically go in', it is not followed by 'into'. It is followed by 'into' when the two words together mean 'begin':

I entered into conversation with the man sitting next to me.

If you are ready to enter into partnership with me, we can start work at once.

379 Hope

Wrong: He hopes of getting a good crop this year.
Correct: He hopes to get a good crop this year.

'Hope' in this example is a verb. It may be followed by 'of' when functioning as a noun:

He has no hope of getting any good crop this year.

380 Inform

Wrong: If you see any strange person, please inform to the police.
Correct: If you see any strange person, please inform the police.

One can 'give information to' someone, but not 'inform to' someone.

381 Lack

Wrong: We lack of many amenities in this town.
Correct: We lack many amenities in this town.

'Lack' is a verb in some contexts, a noun in others. As a verb it is not followed by 'of'.

382 Order

Wrong: You must order for a fresh supply of paper.
Correct: You must order a fresh supply of paper.

'Order', here meaning 'make arrangements to buy', is a verb, and is not followed by 'for'. It can also be a noun with this meaning, and is followed by 'for':

He placed an order for a fresh supply of paper.

'Order' as a verb also means 'command' and is followed by an object + *to* + verb:

The teacher ordered the boy to stand up.

383 Promise

Wrong: I promise of returning the book as soon as I can.

Correct: I promise to return the book as soon as I can.

As a verb, 'promise' is followed by 'to'. It can be followed by 'of' if it functions as a noun, for example:

> He gave the candidate a firm promise of his support.

384 Reach

Wrong: The number of victims of the crash has reached to 200.

Correct: The number of victims of the crash has reached 200.

385 Regret

Wrong: He regretted of not having studied mathematics.

Correct: He regretted not having studied mathematics.

When it means 'feel sorrow over something already done', 'regret' is followed by a noun (including verb-nouns). When it means 'feel sorrow in doing something', 'regret' is followed by *to* + verb:

> I regret to announce the death of an elder statesman.

'Regret' can also be a noun, and may be followed by 'for':

> She showed no regret for her total incompetence.

386 Report

Wrong: They reported of his safe return.
Correct: They reported his safe return.

'Report' can be followed by 'of' if it is used as a noun, for example:

> They presented a report of their findings.

387 Request

Wrong: The carpenter requested for more nails.
Correct: The carpenter requested more nails.

'Request' is a verb in some contexts, a noun in others. As a noun it may be followed by 'for':

> The carpenter submitted a request for more nails.

388 Stress

Wrong: He stressed on the importance of reducing inflation.
Correct: He stressed the importance of reducing inflation.

'Stress' as a verb is followed directly by its object. As a noun it may be followed by 'on':

> He laid stress on the importance of reducing inflation.

389 Summon

Wrong: The Chief summoned for his small boy to come and receive instructions.
Correct: The Chief summoned his small boy to come and receive instructions.

390 Vow

Wrong: She vowed of never seeing him again.
Correct: She vowed never to see him again.

'Vow' is a verb here. It can also be a noun, when it does take 'of':

> Monks have to take vows of poverty, chastity, and obedience.

The wrong Preposition

Included here (numbers 400 to 415) are a number of verbs having the form *be* + adjective + preposition.

391 Arrive

Wrong: Locusts have recently arrived into our district.
or to our district.

Correct: Locusts have recently arrived in our district.

We can say 'come into' or 'come to', but not 'arrive into' or 'arrive to'.

392 Come

Wrong: The Professor came in Zambia in 1975.
Correct: The Professor came to Zambia in 1975.

393 Deal

Wrong: Mrs Rikiya deals on imported goods.
Correct: Mrs Rikiya deals in imported goods.

Deal in' means 'do business in' certain goods; 'deal with' means 'associate with', 'do business with' a person or persons:

> He is very shy, and hardly knows how to deal with other people.

Never use 'on' after 'deal'.

394 Die

Wrong: The old man died because of a heart-attack.
Correct: The old man died of a heart-attack.

'Of' should be used to indicate the physical cause of death.

395 Prepare

Wrong: Ayo is preparing against his brother's wedding.
Correct: Ayo is preparing for his brother's wedding.

396 Result

Wrong: Let's hope the treatment will result on a complete cure *or* will result to a complete cure.

Correct: Let's hope the treatment will result in a complete cure.

397 Share

Wrong: They all want to share of the new amenities being created by the Council.

Correct: They all want to share in the new amenities being created by the Council.

'Share' as a verb meaning 'have a share of' must be followed by 'in', as the correct sentence shows. As a noun it may be followed by 'of':

> I hope soon to receive my share of the profits.

'Share' as a verb followed immediately by an object means 'divide':

> The Government shared the expropriated land among poor farmers.

398 Shout

Wrong: He was shouting on me as if I was deaf.
Correct: He was shouting at me as if I was deaf.

'Shout' is normally followed by 'at', never by 'on'. It is followed by 'to' if it means shouting a particular message, which is stated:

> He shouted to me to stop: I had a flat tyre.

399 Start

Wrong: Portuguese overseas exploration started from the fifteenth century.

Correct: Portuguese overseas exploration started in the fifteenth century.

Something starts at a certain point in time, and if this is a year or a century, the preposition to be used is 'in'. 'From' marks the beginning of a period:

> The Nigerian First Republic lasted from 1960 to 1966.

400 Absorbed

Wrong: Sam was completely absorbed by his studies.
Correct: Sam was completely absorbed in his studies.

'Absorbed by' is mainly used to describe processes in biology and chemistry. 'Absorbed in' is the right expression for being devoted to a task, like studies.

401 Accustomed
Wrong: My father is not accustomed with *or* not accustomed of being addressed as 'sir'.
Correct: My father is not accustomed to being addressed as 'sir'.

402 Afraid
Wrong: Adebola was very afraid from his father.
Correct: Adebola was very afraid of his father.

Wrong: He was always afraid from entering his father's room.
Correct: He was always afraid to enter his father's room.

403 Angry
Wrong: My cousin was very angry from his wife.
Correct: My cousin was very angry with his wife.

Wrong: He was angry of hearing how much money she had spent.
Correct: He was angry at hearing *or* He was angry to hear how much money she had spent.

The rule here is: angry *with* someone; angry *at* something; angry *to* + verb.

404 Annoyed
Wrong: I was annoyed of not finding you in your office.
Correct: I was annoyed at not finding *or* I was annoyed not to find you in your office.

Say 'annoyed with' when a personal noun follows; 'for' can then introduce the reason for the annoyance:

> She was very annoyed with him for the rude way he spoke to her.

405 Ashamed

Wrong: I was ashamed because of you; you did not allow anyone else to speak.

Correct: I was ashamed of you; you did not allow anyone else to speak.

The rule with 'ashamed' is: ashamed *of* somebody; ashamed *at* something, or *to* + verb.

406 Convinced

Wrong: I was not at all convinced with their argument.

Correct: I was not at all convinced by their argument.

Also see number 501.

407 Disgusted

Wrong: I was disgusted of his behaviour towards his wife.

Correct: I was disgusted at *or* disgusted by his behaviour towards his wife.

One is disgusted *at* or *by* something; or *with* somebody:

I was disgusted with him when I heard the full story.

408 Entitled

Wrong: You are not entitled for any increment this year.

Correct: You are not entitled to any increment this year.

While 'entitled for' is wrong, 'due for' is correct:

You are not due for any increment this year.

409 Full

Wrong: These potatoes are full with maggots.

Correct: These potatoes are full of maggots.

410 Interested

Wrong: Francis seems to be very interested on Judith.

Correct: Francis seems to be very interested in Judith.

411 Made

Wrong: The beads were made from coral.
Correct: The beads were made of coral.

'Of' is the preposition required to introduce the *material* out of which something is made. 'From' may be used when a number of different parts are assembled to make something:

> The Chief's headdress was made of coral beads *or* from coral beads.

412 Married

Wrong: Clare is married with a rich businessman.
Correct: Clare is married to a rich businessman.

Also see number 219.

413 Related

Wrong: She is related with the royal family of Tokumo.
Correct: She is related to the royal family of Tokumo.

414 Serious

Wrong: He was very serious on Fatima, and resolved to marry her.
Correct: He was very serious about Fatima, and resolved to marry her.

One is serious (meaning 'deeply interested') *about* somebody; one is serious *with* something, such as an important task:

> He is very serious with his studies nowadays.

415 Surprised

Wrong: We were surprised of his strange behaviour.
Correct: We were surprised at his strange behaviour *or* by his strange behaviour.

Now do Exercises 40 and 41.

10 Verb Patterns

Many common errors result from failure to select the right pattern of words to use after a particular verb. Verbs can be grouped according to the pattern required, as follows:

1 LINKING VERBS. These are verbs which link the subject with its complement: *be, seem, look, feel, become, taste,* etc. The complement may be
   (a) a noun phrase, e.g. He is *a Nigerian.*
   (b) an adjective or adjectival phrase: I feel *hungry*; He is *angry with you*; It is *difficult to find him.*
   (c) a *that*-clause: It appears *that she has returned.*
   (d) an adverbial: He is *at home.*

2 VERBS WITH ONE OBJECT. The object may be
   (a) a noun phrase: He wrote *the letter.*
   (b) a *that*-clause: You said *that I could go.*
   (c) *to* + infinitive: He wants *to go.*
   (d) an *-ing* participle: She likes *sewing.*
   (e) *to* + infinitive preceded by a subject: He wanted *me to come.*
   (f) infinitive without *to*, preceded by a subject: He made *me come.*
   (g) an *-ing* participle preceded by a subject: We heard *him singing.*
   (h) an *-ed* participle preceded by a subject: He got *the job finished.*

3 VERBS WITH TWO OBJECTS. The main patterns are
   (a) indirect object + direct object: He gave *me some money* (*me* – indirect object; *some money* – direct object).
   (b) object + preposition + object of preposition:
   I supply *the College with eggs*; also: I supply *eggs to the College.*

(c) noun phrase + *that*-clause: You told *me that you were leaving*.

4 VERBS WITH OBJECT AND OBJECT COMPLEMENT. The complement may be
   (a) a noun phrase: They elected him *President*.
   (b) an adjective or adjective phrase: They thought him *very rude*.
   (c) *as* or *for* + noun phrase: They regarded him *as a fool*; They mistook him *for a thief*.
   (d) *as* + adjective: He considered the battle *as won*.

5 VERBS WITH NO OBJECT, e.g.
   Rain is falling. My father has arrived.

Verbs with objects are sometimes called TRANSITIVE verbs; verbs with no objects INTRANSITIVE verbs.

Errors with Linking Verbs

416 Wrong omission of **am, is, are**, etc. before Adjectives

Wrong: I happy to write you this letter.
Correct: I am happy to write you this letter.

Wrong: She afraid to report the matter to you.
Correct: She is afraid to report the matter to you.

This is a very elementary error.

417 Wrong use of adverbs after **taste**
Wrong: This cake tastes very sweetly.
Correct: This cake tastes very sweet.

Wrong choice of Object Type

The errors here lie in confusing one type of object with another from the list given in section 2 on page 129.

Wrong use of that-*clause:*

418 Like
Wrong: Mr Rose doesn't like that you visit him at home.

Correct: Mr Rose doesn't like you to visit him at home *or* you visiting him at home *or* your visiting him at home.

The verb 'like' can also be used with nouns and with infinitives:

> I don't like swimming.
> I don't like to swim in a crowded pool.

419 Want

Wrong: Shaibu wants that I lend him my radio-cassette.

Correct: Shaibu wants me to lend him my radio-cassette.

Wrong: Titi wanted that he should buy her a gold necklace.

Correct: Titi wanted him to buy her a gold necklace.

Wrong use of to + *verb (infinitive):*

420 Avoid

Wrong: We can't avoid to mix with people we don't like.

Correct: We can't avoid mixing with people we don't like.

421 Finish

Wrong: Amina finished to type her essay this afternoon.

Correct: Amina finished typing her essay this afternoon.

422 Keep

Wrong: Ada keeps to make excuses for her lateness.

Correct: Ada keeps making *or* keeps on making excuses for her lateness.

'Keep' is followed by *to* if it is then followed by a noun, for example:

> He doesn't always keep to time. (He is not always punctual.)

Keep to the right; you may have an accident.
(Drive more on the right-hand side.)

423 Know

Wrong: The pilot doesn't know to swim.
Correct: The pilot doesn't know how to swim.

Wrong: The nurse doesn't know to speak Luganda.
Correct: The nurse doesn't know how to speak
Luganda.

424 Mind

Wrong: I don't mind to give you a room in my house.
Correct: I don't mind giving you a room in my house.

'Mind' here means 'oppose', 'object to', and is a verb. As
a noun, 'mind' is used in various idioms and it is followed
by *to* + verb:

He could't make up his mind to ask for her
friendship. (He couldn't decide.)
I have had it in mind to visit you at home. (I
have had the intention.)
I have a good mind to punish him for his insol-
ence. (I have a strong desire.)

425 Resist

Wrong: They resisted to have their land taken away
from them.
Correct: They resisted having their land taken away
from them.

Wrong: They resisted him to be transferred to Lagos.
Correct: They resisted his being transferred to Lagos.

'Resist' is never followed by *to*, but directly by nouns
(including verb-nouns). The noun 'resistance', derived
from 'resist', is followed by *to*:

He put up strong resistance to the attempts to
capture him.

426 Stop

Wrong: They told him to stop to introduce irrelevant points.

Correct: They told him to stop introducing irrelevant points.

'Stop' here means 'cease', 'refrain from'. 'Stop' can be followed by *to* in the phrases 'stop to think', 'stop to consider', which means 'reflect before taking action or forming a conclusion':

> He didn't stop to consider whether the boy's story was genuine or not; he gave him a beating at once.

Wrong use of -ing *participle*

427 About

Wrong: He was about entering the hotel when he saw Mr Obe.

Correct: He was about to enter *or* on the point of entering the hotel when he saw Mr Obe.

'About to' meaning 'on the point of' is followed by an infinitive ('enter'); 'on the point of' itself is followed by a verbal noun ('entering').

428 Decide

Wrong: He decided buying a new car to replace his old one.

Correct: He decided to buy *or* He decided on buying a new car to replace his old one.

429 Desire

Wrong: They desire entering university next session.

Correct: They desire to enter university next session.

'Desire' can be either verb or noun. As a verb it can be followed by *to* + verb, or by a noun. As a noun it can be followed by a preposition such as 'to' or 'for'.

430 Refuse

Wrong: The magistrate refused signing any document.
Correct: The magistrate refused to sign any document.

Wrong: Her parents refused her marrying the man of her choice.
Correct: Her parents refused to allow her to marry the man of her choice.

'Refuse' can sometimes be followed just by a noun:

He refused all offers of help.

Wrong use of to + *infinitive preceded by a subject*

431 Appreciate

Wrong: I do not appreciate you to come *or* that you come with all your friends to my house.
Correct: I do not appreciate your coming with all your friends to my house.

432 Make

Wrong: Your story has made me to understand the trouble you are in.
Correct: Your story has made me understand the trouble you are in.

The active form of 'make', meaning 'compel', 'cause', requires the omission of 'to' before the following verbs. But 'to' is required when 'make' is passive:

Through his story I was made to understand the trouble he was in.

433 Prevent

Wrong: He didn't know how to prevent himself to smoke.
Correct: He didn't know how to prevent himself from smoking *or* prevent himself smoking.

434 Suggest

Wrong: I suggested him to raise the matter with the Manager.

Correct: I suggested his raising *or* that he raise *or* that he should raise the matter with the Manager.

Wrong omission of to *before an infinitive:*

435 Allow
Wrong: We do not allow you repeat any examination.
Correct: We do not allow you to repeat any examination.

436 Enable
Wrong: This loan will enable me pay the bride-price.
Correct: This loan will enable me to pay the bride-price.

Wrong use of infinitive instead of -ing *participle:*

437 Be used to
Wrong: I am not yet used to eat heavily three times a day.
Correct: I am not yet used to eating heavily three times a day.

'Be used to' must not be confused with the auxiliary 'used to', which is followed by an infinitive.

438 Look forward to
Wrong: I look forward to see you on your return.
Correct: I look forward to seeing you on your return.

439 Object
Wrong: He strongly objects to be sent to a different school.
Correct: He strongly objects to being sent to a different school.

Wrong: I object him to be interviewed without adequate notice.
Correct: I object to his being interviewed without adequate notice.

Other errors:

440 Expect
Wrong: We do not expect him coming *or* him of
coming till next week.
Correct: We do not expect him to come till next week.

Compare 'expect' with 'suspect' (number 462) 'Expect'
can also be followed by a noun with no following verb:

We are expecting his arrival.

441 Forbid
Wrong: The children were forbidden from playing in
the street.
Correct: The children were forbidden to play in the
street.

Compare 'prevent' (number 433).

442 Wrong use of object + **to** + verb after **instead of**
Wrong: Instead of him to worry about his failure, Isa
ought to have had another try at once.
Correct: Instead of worrying about his failure, Isa
ought to have had another try at once.

Wrong: Instead of them to investigate the matter, the
authorities simply dismissed him.
Correct: Instead of investigating the matter, the
authorities simply dismissed him.

'Rather than' + verb can alternatively be used in the above
examples:

Rather than worry about his failure, Isa ought
to have had another try at once.

Errors in use of two Objects

Wrong use of to *and* for:

443 Bring

Wrong: Bring to me your application form.

Correct: Bring me your application form. *or* Bring your application form to me.

The rule after 'bring' is: *either* indirect object without *to* + direct object; *or* direct object + *to* + indirect object.

Other verbs which behave like 'bring' are: 'lend', 'give', 'grant', 'offer', 'owe', 'pay', 'sell', 'send', 'show', 'tell'.

444 Find

Wrong: My parents said they would find for me a wife.

Correct: My parents said they would find me a wife. *or* a wife for me.

The rule after 'find' is: *either* indirect object without *to* + direct object; *or* direct object + *for* + indirect object.

Other verbs which behave like 'find' are 'make', 'order', and 'reserve'.

Wrong omission of preposition:

445 Provide

Wrong: Are you sure you provided him enough money for his journey?

Correct: Are you sure you provided him with enough money for his journey?

446 Supply

Wrong: They should supply us more stationery.

Correct: They should supply us with more stationery.

447 Two objects wrongly used after **excuse**

Wrong: Excuse me your pen.

Correct: 1 Please let me borrow your pen.

2 Excuse me, may I borrow your pen?

'Excuse me' is a polite way of attracting someone's attention, but it does not convey a request by itself.

Wrong choice of Preposition before Second Object

448 Ask

Wrong: I asked a favour from him.
Correct: 1 I asked a favour of him.
        2 I asked him to do me a favour.

There are actually many ways of continuing a sentence after 'ask', some involving two objects, for example:

I asked a question of him. (Like 'I asked a favour of him.')
I asked him a question. (But not: 'I asked him a favour.')
I asked him the time.
I asked him what the time was.

In these examples 'I' put to 'him' a question, expecting some answer. Another way of using 'ask' is in 'ask for', which means 'seek to obtain', as in these examples:

I asked for my share of the proceeds.
I asked (him) for his help.
I asked for permission to make the journey.
I asked him for a light.

'Ask' can also be followed by 'to' and an infinitive:

I asked to be excused from attending the meeting.
I asked to be allowed to make the journey.

'Ask' here really means 'ask for permission'.

449 Attached

Wrong: Attach this photostat copy with your letter.
Correct: Attach this photostat copy to your letter.

'Attached to' can also mean 'fond of':

She is very attached to her elder brother.

450 Avail

Wrong: I wish to avail the opportunity to meet the Chancellor.

Correct: I wish to avail myself of the opportunity to meet the Chancellor.

The first object after 'avail' is usually a *-self* pronoun: *I availed myself, he availed himself*, etc.

451 Congratulate

Wrong: We congratulated the team for their victory.

Correct: We congratulated the team on their victory.

452 Deprive

Wrong: They deprived him from his membership of the Club.

Correct: They deprived him of his membership of the Club.

453 Do damage, do harm

Wrong: Failure to act decisively will do harm on your reputation *or* do damage on your reputation.

Correct: Failure to act decisively will do harm to your reputation *or* do damage to your reputation.

454 Educate

Wrong: The Secretary should be educated on the responsibilities of his position.

Correct: The Secretary should be educated in the responsibilities of his position.

455 Exchange

Wrong: Okoye wanted to exchange his watch with another one.

Correct: Okoye wanted to exchange his watch for another one.

456 Excuse

Wrong: He felt ill, and asked them to excuse him in the meeting.

Correct: He felt ill, and asked them to excuse him from the meeting.

This means that he asked to be allowed not to attend the meeting. See also number 447.

457 Invest
Wrong: He decided to invest all his money on textiles.
Correct: He decided to invest all his money in textiles.

458 Leave
Wrong: Matthew left Malawi to Zambia in 1975.
Correct: Matthew left Malawi for Zambia in 1975.

459 Prefer
Wrong: I prefer maize than cassava.
Correct: I prefer maize to cassava.

One prefers something *to* something else; one likes something 'better' or 'more' *than* something else:

I like maize more than cassava.

460 Relieve
Wrong: They relieved the defeated General from his command.
Correct: They relieved the defeated General of his command.

461 Substitute
Wrong: The accountant substituted new figures with the old ones.
Correct: The accountant substituted new figures for the old ones.

462 Suspect
Wrong: The police suspected him for being the thief.
Correct: The police suspected him of being the thief.

463 Throw
Wrong: Helen was so angry that she picked up a book and threw it to me.

Correct: Helen was so angry that she picked up a book and threw it at me.

One throws something *to* somebody when the person is expected to catch it.

Wrong use of 'as' before Complement
464 Appoint
Wrong: They appointed him as Chairman of the meeting.
Correct: They appointed him Chairman of the meeting.

Also behaving like 'appoint' are 'elect' and 'consider'. Verbs that do have 'as' in their complement include 'address someone as'; 'refer to someone as'; 'dress as'.

Verbs wrongly used without an Object
465 Disappoint
Wrong: We have fixed the meeting for 10 o'clock. I hope you will not disappoint.
Correct: We have fixed the meeting for 10 o'clock. I hope you will not disappoint us.

466 Enjoy
Wrong: You will enjoy at that place; it has a good social life.
Correct: You will enjoy that place *or* You will enjoy yourself at that place; it has a good social life.

467 Further
Wrong: His ideas are not clear, but he definitely wants to further.
Correct: His ideas are not clear, but he definitely wants to further his education.

Now do Exercise 42.

11 Lexis

Many errors in English are the result of using words that are not suitable to the context in which they are used. Often this means confusing two words that have similar meanings. These are errors of 'lexis', and they will be examined by looking in turn at nouns, adjectives, verbs, and adverbs again. Then follows a section dealing with words confused because of similar sound or spelling.

Nouns confused

468 Academics and studies

Wrong: I am going to become a trader; I don't think I will ever be good in academics.

Correct: I am going to become a trader; I don't think I will ever be good in the academic field *or* be good at studies.

'Academics' does not mean 'academic pursuits' or 'the academic line'; only 'academic people', for example:

> Academics are often accused of being people out of touch with reality.

469 Alphabets and letters

Wrong: Many English words contain more than ten alphabets.

Correct: Many English words contain more than ten letters.

An alphabet is a list of the letters which are used to make up the words of a language:

> The English alphabet contains 26 letters.

470 **Amount** wrongly used
Wrong: I obtained some amount from my father and was able to settle all my debts.
Correct: I obtained some money from my father and was able to settle all my debts.

An 'amount' simply means a quantity. We can speak of an 'amount of paper', 'an amount of repairs', 'an amount of work'. Do not use 'amount' without saying what it is an amount *of*.

471 **Chance** and **room**
Wrong: There was no chance in my car for a fifth person.
Correct: There was no room in my car for a fifth person.

'Room' here just means 'space'. It can be used like this in addition to meaning 'compartment in a house'.

472 **Dresses** and **clothes**
Wrong: All his dresses were destroyed in the fire.
Correct: All his clothes were destroyed in the fire.

'Dresses' are garments worn by women, covering both the upper and the lower parts of the body. 'Clothes' (a plural noun with no singular) are garments in general.

473 **Fellow** wrongly used
Wrong: He met the fellow at the cinema and invited her to his house.
Correct: He met the girl at the cinema and invited her to his house.

'Fellow' can mean 'young man' but not 'girl'. But compounds like 'fellow-students', 'fellow-lecturers', can refer to both males and females.

474 **Friendship** wrongly used after **make**
Wrong: Solomon, I would like to make friendship with you.

Correct: Solomon, I would like to make friends with you.

'Make friends' is an idiom used even when one person is asking for the friendship of just one other person.

475 Hand and wing
Wrong: The bird couldn't fly because its left hand was injured.
Correct: The bird couldn't fly because its left wing was injured.

Birds and animals do not have 'hands'.

476 Heat wrongly used after feel
Wrong: He removed his tie because he was feeling too much heat.
Correct: He removed his tie because he was feeling too hot.

The heat here is not specific. (See page 201.) The definite article is not required, but it is not possible to say 'feel heat'. When the heat is specific, it is possible to say 'feel the heat':

> He was used to the mild climate of the plateau, so when he was sent down to the coast he felt the heat.

477 Kilo wrongly used
Wrong: From here to the next big town is 45 kilos.
Correct: From here to the next big town is 45 kilometres.

The abbreviation 'kilo' should only be used of 'kilogram', not of 'kilometre', for example:

> She bought five kilos of onions.

478 Likeness and liking
Wrong: It is because of my likeness for you that I have invited you.
Correct: It is because of my liking for you that I have invited you.

'Likeness' means 'resemblance', and is followed by 'to'; 'liking' is the right word here, meaning 'love', 'affection'.

479 Management and managing

Wrong: Okoye said his life was one of management, and not yet one of enjoyment.

Correct: Okoye said his life was one of (just) managing, and not yet one of enjoyment.

Both 'managing' and 'management' are derived from the verb 'manage', which has many meanings. Among them are: (1) 'control' or 'direct' (an organization, such as a business); (2) 'barely succeed', 'barely cope' (with problems, with life, etc.). The noun 'management' can only have the first meaning:

> His colleagues in the Production Unit do not admire his style of management.

480 Mum, mummy, mother

Wrong: 'How is your mummy?' the young accountant asked his old teacher.

Correct: 'How is your mother?' the young accountant asked his old teacher.

'Mum' and 'mummy' are endearing ways of addressing or referring to a mother, but 'mummy' is used by small children, and sounds ridiculous when used by an older person referring to the mother of another older person. 'Mum' can be used between equals who are close friends.

Distinguish between the uses of 'dad' and 'daddy' and 'father' in the same way.

481 Poultry wrongly used

Wrong: Sadiku decided to set up a poultry.
Correct: Sadiku decided to set up a poultry-farm.

'Poultry' is an uncountable noun meaning chickens, turkeys, etc. Use it correctly like this:

> He keeps poultry, pigs, and a few sheep.

Adjectives confused

482 Ashamed and shy

Wrong: Akin was very ashamed by nature and never spoke in public.

Correct: Akin was very shy by nature and never spoke in public.

Feeling ashamed means having disturbed emotions because of a sense of guilt over a particular matter.

483 Conducive and agreeable

Wrong: I do not find sleeping in an air-conditioned room conducive.

Correct: I do not find sleeping in an air-conditioned room agreeable.

Always use 'to' after 'conducive', which means 'causing', 'facilitating', for example:

> I do not think that sleeping in a room with all the windows closed is conducive to good health.

484 Elder and elderly

Wrong: 'As you are an elderly person, I am supposed to show you respect,' said the little boy to the young teacher.

Correct: 'As you are an older person, I am supposed to show you respect,' said the little boy to the young teacher.

The meaning of 'elderly' is 'past middle age'; it is a polite way of saying 'old'. But the teacher in the example is young. 'Elder' could be used instead of 'older', but as an adjective it usually occurs in the phrase 'elder brother' or 'elder sister'. 'Elder' also functions as a noun, either singular or plural, meaning 'senior in age or status':

> The elders of our town hold frequent meetings.

485 Far-fetched wrongly used

Wrong: She refused to speak to the other girl, and the reason is not far-fetched.

146

Correct: She refused to speak to the other girl, and the reason is not hard to find.

'Far-fetched' cannot be used to mean 'hard for any reasonable person to find', which is surely the meaning required here. 'Far-fetched' means 'bizarre', 'unusual', and is used, often with disapproval, to describe plans or ideas that are beyond the imagination of ordinary people:

> His plans to turn this wilderness into an industrial complex are quite far-fetched.

486 Fatal and serious

Wrong: He suffered a fatal accident, and was rushed to hospital, but later recovered.

Correct: He suffered a serious accident, and was rushed to hospital, but later recovered.

'Fatal' means 'resulting in death'; we could use it correctly like this:

> He suffered a fatal accident. May his soul rest in peace.

487 Lovely and loving

Wrong: This is your lovely son writing to you.
Correct: This is your loving son writing to you.

'Lovely' means 'beautiful'; 'loving' means 'affectionate', 'having love'.

488 Popular and widespread

Wrong: Smallpox used to be a popular disease in many parts of the world.

Correct: Smallpox used to be a common disease *or* a widespread disease in many parts of the world.

The most frequent meaning of 'popular' is not 'pertaining to many people' but 'liked by many people', for example:

> The music of Bob Marley is popular with black youth throughout the world.

489 Rampant wrongly used

Wrong: The buying of newspapers has become rampant in Nigeria, and it is the ideal way of finding out what is happening in the country.

Correct: The buying of newspapers has become widespread *or* has become popular in Nigeria, and it is the ideal way of finding out what is happening in the country.

'Rampant' means 'widespread', but is only used to describe something of which one disapproves:

I am afraid that examination malpractices have become rampant in higher institutions.

490 Second and following

Wrong: He was admitted to hospital, and on the second day they operated on him.

Correct: He was admitted to hospital, and on the following day they operated on him.

Use 'the second day' only when a series of several days is being thought of, and there is interest in knowing what happened on a particular day in the series:

It was on the second day of the festival that the police had to intervene.

491 Strong and tough

Wrong: I can't eat this meat; it is too strong.
Correct: I can't eat this meat; it is too tough.

'Tough' is the right word here meaning 'difficult to chew'.

492 Sweet and tasty

Wrong: That chicken we ate was very sweet.
Correct: That chicken we ate was very tasty.

Like 'tasty', 'sweet' means 'having an agreeable taste', but 'sweet' is used for sugary things. See also number 417.

Verbs confused

493 Accept and agree

Wrong: I accept to accompany you as far as the bridge.

Correct: I agree to accompany you as far as the bridge.

'Agree', but not 'accept' is followed by 'to'. 'Accept' means 'willingly receive something offered'; 'agree' means 'willingly do what one is asked to do', or 'give the assent of one's judgment' to some statement.

494 Answer and be called

Wrong: He doesn't answer 'Benson'; that's his brother's name.

Correct: 1 He doesn't answer to the name (of) 'Benson'; that's his brother's name.

2 He isn't called 'Benson'; that's his brother's name.

3 His name isn't 'Benson'; that's his brother's name.

495 Be beaten wrongly used with rain

Wrong: I was beaten by the rain on my way home.

Correct: I was caught in the rain on my way home.

496 Borrow and lend

Wrong: I would like you to borrow me fifty shillings.

Correct: 1 I would like you to lend me fifty shillings.

2 I would like to borrow fifty shillings from you.

The two correct sentences have the same meaning.

497 Buy and pay for

Wrong: How much did you buy that camera?

Correct: How much did you pay for that camera?

'Buy' can also be used in talking of the price if it is followed by 'for' coming after the object:

He bought his camera for two hundred pounds.

But 'pay for' is just as correct; and note the order of the words:

> He paid two hundred pounds for his camera.

498 Capture wrongly used

Wrong: In 1935 the Italians captured Ethiopia.
Correct: In 1935 the Italians invaded Ethiopia.

Ethiopia is a country, not a city; therefore it cannot be captured. 'Capture' can be used for the seizure of a town or city, or a person. The word for the successful taking of a whole country is 'overrun' or 'conquer', and for the beginning of the process, 'invade'.

499 Carry and take

Wrong: There goes a taxi that will carry you to the airport.

Correct: There goes a taxi that will take *or* convey you to the airport.

500 Continue and keep on

Wrong: I had never seen the man before, but he continued telling me how we had played football together as kids.

Correct: I had never seen the man before, but he kept telling me *or* kept on telling me how we had played football together as kids.

You can only continue doing something if you were doing it before and then stopped, after which you continued. For example:

> He stopped and looked around to see if people were listening. Then he continued the lecture.

'Continually' can be used instead of 'keep (on)' to give the sense of 'again and again':

> She was continually complaining about her daughter-in-law.

501 **Convince** and **persuade**

Wrong: I convinced her to go back to her mother's house.

Correct: I persuaded her to go back to her mother's house.

We persuade someone *to* do something, we convince someone *that* something, or *of* something, for example:

> I convinced her that it was in her best interest to go back to her mother's house.

502 **Discover** and **invent**

Wrong: Printing was originally discovered by the Chinese.

Correct: Printing was originally invented by the Chinese.

We 'discover' something which was already in existence before the discovery:

> Columbus discovered America.
> Sir Alexander Fleming discovered penicillin.

503 **Drive** and **dismiss**

Wrong: We had to drive the fellow in the end; he was very unreliable.

Correct: We had to dismiss the fellow *or* sack the fellow in the end; he was very unreliable.

'Drive' cannot be used to mean 'terminate the employment of'. 'Sack' used in this sense is very colloquial.

504 **Favour** wrongly used

Wrong: The result did not favour me. I had only an ordinary pass.

Correct: My result was not good. I had only an ordinary pass.

'Favour' used as a verb must have a human subject.

505 Follow and accompany

Wrong: I will follow you to Ilorin if there is room in your car.

Correct: I will accompany you to Ilorin if there is room in your car.

'Follow' means 'go behind', not 'go with' somebody.

506 Forget and leave

Wrong: I must have forgotten my book in the hostel.

Correct: I must have left my book in the hostel.

To forget something means that that thing is no longer in one's memory, for example:

I forget where I put my book.

507 Hear and listen

Example: A: You don't follow what I am saying.

Wrong: B: I am hearing you.

Correct: B: I am listening to you.

Speaker 'B' is no doubt listening to Speaker 'A', that is, paying attention to what 'A' is saying even if he doesn't understand. 'Hear' simply means that the ears are registering sounds. Part of a conversation on the phone might be:

A: The line is very bad tonight.

B: Yes, I can only just hear you.

Avoid using the continuous forms of 'hear'; use 'can' or 'could' instead. Also see number 183.

508 Hear and smell

Wrong: I can hear the smell of gas.

Correct: I can smell gas.

One cannot hear a smell, only a sound. 'Smell' is a noun in some contexts, a verb in others. If a noun is desired in the above sentence, say

I can detect the smell of gas.

152

509 Wrong use of **help**

Wrong: Please help me pick up that piece of paper.

'Help' normally means to provide the aid needed by a person if his own efforts are not sufficient to achieve his objective. The above sentence suggests that two people are needed to pick up a piece of paper, which is rather odd. Say instead

Please pick up that piece of paper for me.

For + object can often be used at the end of a sentence like this instead of 'help' + object at the beginning. If you must use 'help' say this:

Please help me and pick up that piece of paper.

510 **Hire** and **rent**

Wrong: He hires this house from Alhaji Suberu.
Correct: He rents this house from Alhaji Suberu.

'Hire' is used for something portable or mobile; a car, a loudspeaker system. One can also speak of hiring persons: labourers, for example.

511 **Hope, think,** and **wish**

Wrong: I hope this chair will soon collapse; you had better call a carpenter at once to repair it.
Correct: I think this chair will soon collapse; you had better call a carpenter at once to repair it.

Clearly the speaker does not want the chair to collapse; therefore he cannot 'hope' it will collapse.

Wrong: So you are standing for election? I wish you succeed.
Correct: So you are standing for election? I hope (that) you succeed *or* I wish you success.

The Present Simple Tense ('succeed') cannot be used in the clause that follows 'wish'. The alternatives in this example are to use the Present Simple, preceded by 'hope'; or 'wish', followed by the objects 'you' and 'success'.

153

512 Lay and lie

Wrong: I told Onuoha to lay down and rest.
Correct: I told Onuoha to lie down and rest.

'Lie' means (1) 'speak falsely'; (2) 'repose'. 'Lay' means 'put':

>She was told to lay her needlework on the table.

The two words are often confused because the parts of 'lie' meaning 'repose' are *lie – lay – lain*, while the parts of 'lay' are *lay – laid – laid*. Using 'lie' in the Past Simple Tense we can say

>Onuoha lay down for half an hour. (He rested.)

513 Learn and teach

Wrong: I want you to learn me how to grow corn.
Correct: I want you to teach me how to grow corn.

'Learn' cannot be followed by a personal object. 'Teach' means 'make someone learn'.

514 Leave and give up

Wrong: You should leave smoking; it will damage your health.
Correct: You should give up smoking *or* stop smoking *or* leave off smoking; it will damage your health.

'Leave' as a verb means 'go away' from someone or something which remains in place.

515 Like to and want to

Wrong: I like to have my dinner now.
Correct: I want to have my dinner now.

The word 'now' shows that the speaker is expressing a desire for his dinner at the moment of speaking; for this, 'want' must be used. 'Like' would express a general desire or liking:

>I like to have my dinner early; but it's already 12.30, and where is the cook?

516 Maintain and repair

Wrong: The suspension of this car is bad; I must go and maintain it.

Correct: The suspension of this car is bad; I must go and repair it.

'Maintain' means taking steps to keep something in a decent working condition even when nothing is apparently wrong with it. Many repairs would not be necessary if a machine such as a car were properly maintained.

517 Make and take

Wrong: Maika is to make his first examination on May 31st.

Correct: Maika is to take his first examination on May 31st.

Note various uses of 'take' and 'make':

> *take* an examination, a test, a decision, an oath, a photo, time (take time = delay), offence (take offence = be offended);
>
> *make* an attempt, an effort, a mess, a fuss, a promise, a sketch (or *do* a sketch), a survey (or *do* a survey), a purchase, a gain, sense, profit, plans.

518 Make wrongly used with accident, operation

Wrong: He made an accident on the motorway.

Correct: He had an accident on the motorway.

Wrong: She went into hospital to make an operation.

Correct: She went into hospital to have an operation.

519 March and tread

Wrong: Mrs Oke marched on an enormous scorpion.

Correct: Mrs Oke trod on an enormous scorpion.

'Tread' means 'put one's foot down, with force'. 'March' means 'walk with regular, forceful steps', like a soldier.

520 Meet wrongly used with absent, absence

Wrong: They came to my house, but met my absence *or* met me absent.

Correct: They came to my house, but found me absent.

521 **Name** and **nominate**
Wrong: They named him to do a course in America.
Correct: They nominated him to do a course in America.

'Nominate' also has to do with naming, but it means 'propose the name of someone' for some official function. The verb 'name' means 'give a name to' (a new-born child, for example), or 'cite':

> He named one of his colleagues before the court as his wife's lover.

522 **Neglect** and **ignore**
Wrong: Ola once more began to complain about his in-laws, but this time his wife neglected him.
Correct: Ola once more began to complain about his in-laws, but this time his wife ignored him.

'Ignore' is the word meaning 'deliberately not attend to'. 'Neglect' means 'leave unattended to', not at a particular moment.

523 **Occasion** and **opportunity**
Wrong: I was so busy that I simply did not have any occasion to go to the bank.
Correct: I was so busy that I simply did not have any opportunity to go to the bank.

'Opportunity' means 'time' or 'moment' that can be used profitably. 'Occasion' just means a certain time, but also a special or important time, for example:

> Carnival time is a great occasion in the year for West Indians.

524 **Overrun** and **run over**
Wrong: One day you will be overrun by a passing car.
Correct: One day you will be run over by a passing car.

'Overrun' is used to describe an army quickly moving over and taking possession of an area.

525 Pain and hurt

Wrong: My leg is paining me; I must go to see a doctor.

Correct: My leg is painful *or* is hurting *or* is hurting me; I must go to see a doctor.

'Pain' as a verb means 'cause distress' – of a psychological rather than a physical sort. It is commonly used with an impersonal subject:

It pains me to hear that you have squandered all the money I gave you.

526 Promise and intend

Wrong: I promise to start trading next year, but I haven't yet told my wife about it.

Correct: I intend to start trading next year, but I haven't yet told my wife about it.

'Promise' is an assurance one gives to someone else.

527 Put and make

Wrong: The actual amount is 998.94. Put it 1000 as a round figure.

Correct: The actual amount is 998.94. Make it 1000 as a round figure.

528 Raise and rise confused

Wrong: The sun raises in the east.
Correct: The sun rises in the east.

'Rise' means 'go up', 'come up'; 'raise' means 'bring up'.

529 Refuse wrongly used

Wrong: I have refilled the stove, but it still refuses to light.

Correct: I have refilled the stove, but it still won't light *or* it still doesn't light.

You are advised to avoid using 'refuse' with subjects other than human beings and animals, such as 'stove' 'door', etc.

530 **Remember** and **remind**

Wrong: Please remember me to buy more fuel.
Correct: Please remind me to buy more fuel.

'Remember' cannot take an object before 'to' except when it means 'send greetings from', for example:

Please remember me to your parents.

531 **Rob** and **steal**

Wrong: Someone robbed my watch as I was entering a bus.
Correct: Someone robbed me of my watch *or* stole my watch from me as I was entering a bus.

The rule is: 'rob' someone *of* something, 'steal' something *from* someone.

532 **Scrape** and **shave**

Wrong: Dauda decided to scrape off his beard.
Correct: Dauda decided to shave off his beard.

'Scrape' is used to describe the removing of rather solid or viscous materials, like mud, paint, etc. 'Shave' is the word used for hair when it is to be removed from its roots.

533 **Seize, cease,** and **cut off**

Wrong: The Power Authority have seized *or* ceased our electricity supply because you have not paid the bill.
Correct: The Power Authority have stopped *or* disconnected *or* cut off our electricity supply because you have not paid the bill.

'Cease' is not normally followed by a noun object. 'Seize' here would mean that the Power Authority grabbed the electricity supply and held it by force. Also see number 556.

534 **Size** and **fit**

Wrong: I could not buy those shoes; they did not size me.

Correct: I could not buy those shoes; they did not fit me *or* they were not my size.

'Size' cannot be used as a verb, only as a noun.

535 **Take** and **come**

Wrong: Tunde took fifth in the 100 metres.
Correct: Tunde came fifth in the 100 metres.

536 **Take in** and **conceive**

Wrong: They were married in October and in November she took in.

Correct: They were married in October and in November she conceived.

'Take in' has many meanings, but using it to mean 'conceive' is not Standard English.

537 **Take** wrongly used with **cold**

Wrong: You had better put on a sweater, or you will take cold.

Correct: You had better put on a sweater, or you will catch cold.

538 **Take** wrongly used with **sick**

Wrong: He has taken sick, and has not been here for two days.

Correct: He has fallen sick, and has not been here for two days.

'Take' cannot be used in the active in this example, but it can be used in the passive:

> He has been taken sick, and has not been here for two days.

539 **Take** wrongly used with **example**

Wrong: If you take example from him, you will never find yourself in difficulties.

Correct: If you follow his example, you will never find yourself in difficulties.

159

540 Uncover and discover

Wrong: They saw his footprints and finally uncovered him in the barn.

Correct: They saw his footprints and finally discovered him in the barn.

'Uncover' means 'remove the cover of'. The meaning here is that they found someone who was hiding from them.

541 Use, keep, and spend

Wrong: He used *or* He kept three weeks in his home town.

Correct: He spent three weeks in his home town.

It is correct to speak of 'spending' time, as well as money. 'Use' when it has 'time' as an object means 'use for a certain purpose':

> He uses all his spare time to better his athletic performance.

542 Want and try wrongly used

Wrong: The wheel wanted *or* was trying to come loose, so I stopped the car and tightened it.

Correct: The wheel was coming loose, so I stopped the car and tightened it.

In English only human subjects can want or try to do something. Also see number 529.

543 Win and beat

Wrong: Saidu won me three games of chess.

Correct: 1 Saidu won three games of chess against me.

2 Saidu beat me three times at chess.

'Win' cannot be followed by an indirect object ('me') indicating the person defeated; 'beat' must be used instead. 'Won' can be followed by a direct object indicating the contest; 'beat' cannot.

Verbs with redundant words or phrases

544 Deliver

Wrong: The woman was in labour for many hours; she finally delivered her baby just after midnight.

Correct: The woman was in labour for many hours; she finally delivered just after midnight.

In this context 'deliver' can, and should, be used with no object following; the woman could not deliver anything else but a baby.

545 Get up

Wrong: I get up from my bed at 7.30, have a bath, and eat my breakfast.

Correct: I get up at 7.30, have a bath, and eat my breakfast.

When 'get up' clearly means 'leave one's bed', it is not necessary to add the phrase 'from my (his, etc.) bed'.

546 Wave

Wrong: I waved my hand to him but he didn't see me.

Correct: I waved to him but he didn't see me.

'Wave' by itself means 'wave one's hand' to attract attention or in greeting, so it is not necessary to add the words 'my hand'. If something other than one's hand is waved, then it must be mentioned:

> The children waved their flags vigorously.
> He was waving a paper at me; he seemed to be very angry.

Adverbs confused

547 At last

Wrong: The surgeon fought hard to save my sister's life, but she died at last.

Correct: 1 The surgeon fought hard to save my sister's life, but she died in the end.

2 The surgeon fought hard to save my sister's life, but she finally died.

'At last' is normally used when something desirable happens for which one has been waiting a long time:

At last we saw his car on the horizon, and there were loud cheers.
I reached home at last, very tired after a journey of many hours.

'Finally' or 'in the end' can be used whether what happens is desirable or not.

548 Conclusively and in conclusion
Wrong: Conclusively, there are three main vegetation zones in Nigeria.
Correct: In conclusion, there are three main vegetation zones in Nigeria.

'Conclusively' does not mean 'finally' or 'in conclusion', but 'decisively', 'convincingly'.

Galileo demonstrated conclusively that the earth is round.

549 Late and lately
Wrong: Mr Azi always comes to work lately.
Correct: Mr Azi always come to work late.

'Lately' means 'recently':

I haven't seen the Emir lately *or* recently.

Words confused because of similar sound or spelling

Some pairs of words are easily confused because they are pronounced similarly or spelled similarly. In what follows, phonetic symbols are occasionally introduced to help users of this book who may be familiar with them, and a full list of these is given on pages 231–2.

550 Accession and ascension

Wrong: On his ascension to the throne the King granted a general pardon.

Correct: On his accession to the throne the King granted a general pardon.

'Ascension' means 'going up' in the physical sense, for example:

Christians and Moslems alike believe in the ascension of Jesus into heaven.

551 Advice and advise

Wrong: I adviced her to pay heed to his words.

Correct: I advised her to pay heed to his words.

'Advise' is the verb, 'advice' the noun. The sound of the 's' in 'advise' is /z/; the sound of 'c' in 'advice' is /s/.

552 Belief and believe

Wrong: He acted in the believe that he was right.

Correct: He acted in the belief that he was right.

'Believe' is a verb, 'belief' a noun.

553 Been and being

Wrong: The matter has being reported to me.

Correct: The matter has been reported to me.

Wrong: The rumour is been investigated.

Correct: The rumour is being investigated.

Wrong: I am looking forward to been promoted.

Correct: I am looking forward to being promoted.

Wrong: Been the Acting Vice-Chancellor was not an easy job for him.

Correct: Being the Acting Vice-Chancellor was not an easy job for him.

'Been' is pronounced /biːn/; 'being' is pronounced /biːɪŋ/, and can be thought of as two parts or syllables, 'be-ing'.

So much for pronunciation. In terms of function in sentences the difference is this: *been* (past participle of *be*) can only be used after 'have', 'has', 'had', 'having'. *Being* (present participle and verb-noun) is used (i) after 'am', 'is', 'are', 'was', 'were'; or (ii) at the beginning of a sentence or clause; or (iii) after a preposition.

554 **Border** and **boarder**

Wrong: He was approaching the boarder between
Nigeria and Benin.

Correct: He was approaching the border between
Nigeria and Benin.

A 'border' is the dividing line between one area and another; a 'boarder' is a person who lodges in a place, like students who live in a College and are fed there.

555 **Cause** and **course**

Wrong: The Lieutenant was killed in the cause of the
fighting.

Correct: The Lieutenant was killed in the course of the
fighting.

'Cause' (with the 's' pronounced /z/) and 'course' (with the 's' pronounced /s/) are often used in the same context. 'Cause' means 'reason behind' something; 'course' means 'duration', 'process' etc.

556 **Cease** and **seize**

Wrong: He was ordered to seize smoking immediately.
Correct: He was ordered to cease smoking immediately.

'Cease' (with the 's' pronounced /s/) means 'stop'; 'seize' means 'grab', 'hold by force'. Also see number 533.

557 **Complain** and **Complaint**

Wrong: Someone has brought a complain against you.
Correct: Someone has brought a complaint against you.

The difference here is simply that 'complain' is a verb, 'complaint' is a noun.

558 **Economic** and **economy**

Wrong: What steps are they taking to improve the country's economic?

Correct: What steps are they taking to improve the country's economy?

'Economy' is a noun, as required here; 'economic' is an adjective.

559 **Fate** and **faith**

Wrong: Ameh is just wasting his life; I don't know what his faith will be.

Correct: Ameh is just wasting his life; I don't know what his fate will be.

Wrong: My fate in him has been much reduced.

Correct: My faith in him has been much reduced.

These two words are easily confused because of similar sound and because both can be used in a religious or philosophical context. 'Fate' means 'destiny' or 'future condition'; 'faith' means 'belief', 'confidence'.

560 **Given** and **giving**

Wrong: We have been giving our allowance, but they haven't yet got theirs.

Correct: We have been given our allowance, but they haven't yet got theirs.

Wrong: They have been given out regular bulletins.

Correct: They have been giving out regular bulletins.

In the first example 'given' is required; 'we have been giving' would mean that we gave our allowances to somebody. The Present Perfect Passive, not the Present Continuous Active, is required. In the second example it is the Present Perfect Continuous active that is required.

561 **Guard** and **guide**

Wrong: It is a ruler's duty to guide his people against any misfortune.

Correct: It is a ruler's duty to guard his people against any misfortune.

These two words are easily confused because they occur in the same context. A ruler's duty may be to 'guide' as well as to 'guard' his people. 'Guard' however means 'protect' and is followed by 'against' or 'from' something unpleasant; while 'guide' means 'direct the course of'. 'Guard' is clearly the right word here.

562 Had and heard
Wrong: I had that he had been unconscious.
Correct: I heard that he had been unconscious.

563 Independent and independence
Wrong: Tanzania obtained its independent in 1961.
Correct: Tanzania obtained its independence in 1961.

The noun is 'independence'; 'independent' is the adjective.

564 Junction and juncture
Wrong: The Army now made rapid progress, and victory was certain. At that junction the Prime Minister resigned.
Correct: The Army now made rapid progress, and victory was certain. At that juncture the Prime Minister resigned.

Both these words fundamentally mean 'joining'. But 'junction' normally means a place where two or more lines meet, such as railway lines or electric wires. 'Juncture' means 'coming together of events', in other words 'time' or 'moment'.

565 Knees and kneels
Wrong: He was on his kneels begging to be forgiven.
Correct: He was on his knees begging to be forgiven.

'Kneels' is a verb, meaning 'go down on one's knees'.

566 **Live** and **leave**

Wrong: Isaac has been leaving with his brother for six
months.

Correct: Isaac has been living with his brother for six
months.

'Live' means 'dwell' or 'be alive'; 'leave' means 'depart
from'.

567 **Lose** and **loose; lost** and **loosed**

Wrong: If you loose this pen, I will not buy you
another one.

Correct: If you lose this pen, I will not buy you
another one.

Wrong: He loosed his glasses on his last visit to
Lusaka.

Correct: He lost his glasses on his last visit to Lusaka.

'Lose' means 'not find', and its parts are: *lose – lost – lost*.
'Loose' means 'untie', 'release', and its parts are: *loose –
loosed – loosed*.

568 **Loss** and **lost**

Wrong: He was depressed by the lost of his passport.
Correct: He was depressed by the loss of his passport.

'Loss', which is required here, is a noun related to the
verb 'lose'. 'Lost', as number 567 shows, is the Past
Simple tense of 'lose'.

569 **Match** and **march**

Wrong: The soldiers were ordered to start matching.
Correct: The soldiers were ordered to start marching.

570 **Nationalize** and **naturalize**

Wrong: Mr Smith is a nationalized Nigerian.
Correct: Mr Smith is a naturalized Nigerian.

'Naturalized' is the right word meaning 'be admitted to
citizenship' of a country; 'nationalize' means 'make
national property'.

571 **Order** and **other**

Wrong: He went to Kaduna in other to visit an eye specialist.

Correct: He went to Kaduna in order to visit an eye specialist.

There is no phrase 'in other to'. 'Order' is a noun, 'other' an adjective.

572 **Owe** and **own**

Wrong: You are free to go, since you do not own us anything.

Correct: You are free to go, since you do not owe us anything.

'Own' means 'possess'; 'owe' means 'have something to repay to' (somebody).

573 **Pack** and **park**

Wrong: Rahimi was told to park his belongings and vacate the room at once.

Correct: Rahimi was told to pack his belongings and vacate the room at once.

These are two more words with similar sound and often used in the same context. 'Park' is normally used with vehicles, and means 'station temporarily'; 'pack' means 'gather together in a bundle', 'wrap', 'fill a container with'.

574 **Price** and **prize**

Wrong: Satisfaction is the price of success.
Correct: Satisfaction is the prize of success.

Wrong: He paid a heavy prize for his rejection of their demands.

Correct: He paid a heavy price for his rejection of their demands.

'Price' (with the 's' pronounced /s/) and 'prize' are easily confused because of similar sound and similar meaning, and because they occur in similar contexts. 'Prize' means 'reward', sometimes in the form of money, and this is the meaning required in the first example; success brings a reward in the form of satisfaction. 'Price' means 'cost', or the money for which something is bought or sold. This is the meaning required in the second example; his rejection of their demands cost him dearly – perhaps he later lost his position, or even his life.

575 **Proof** and **prove**
Wrong: They dropped the case for lack of prove.
Correct: They dropped the case for lack of proof.

'Prove' is a verb, 'proof' the corresponding noun.

576 **Quiet** and **quite**
Wrong: My father is not quiet sound in health.
Correct: My father is not quite sound in health.

'Quite', an adverb of degree (see number 319), is the right word here. 'Quiet' is an adjective meaning 'not making a noise'.

577 **Safe** and **save**
Wrong: I wish you a save journey.
Correct: I wish you a safe journey.

Wrong: May God safe you from all ill.
Correct: May God save you from all ill.

'Save' is a verb, 'safe' is an adjective.

578 **Sale** and **sell**
Wrong: His old car is now up for sell.
Correct: His old car is now up for sale.

Both 'sale', and 'sell' have to do with selling; but 'sell' is a verb, while 'sale' is a noun and therefore required after the preposition 'for'.

579 **Section** and **session**
Wrong: In the afternoon section I only teach Health Science.
Correct: In the afternoon session I only teach Health Science.

A section is usually a part of something that occupies space: a section of a room, a building, a city, a community, a book, a drawer, etc. A session is a meeting or a period during which people meet or come together. This is the right word to use here for an overcrowded school where some students have their lessons in the morning and others in the afternoon.

580 Seen and seeing

Wrong: I have just seeing a wonderful film.
Correct: I have just seen a wonderful film.

The past participle of 'see' is 'seen', which is required after 'have'. 'Seeing' can never be used after 'have'. Also see number 553.

581 Sight, site, and cite

Wrong: They cited *or* they sighted the factory in the wrong place; there's no water near by.
Correct: They sited the factory in the wrong place; there's no water nearby.

'Sight', both verb and noun, has to do with seeing; 'site' means 'place' or 'situate'. 'Cite', pronounced in exactly the same way as 'sight' and 'site', means 'quote'.

582 Sit and seat

Wrong: Mr Chukwu took his sit at the table.
Correct: Mr Chukwu took his seat at the table.

'Sit' is always a verb and never a noun. 'Seat' is sometimes a noun, sometimes a verb; as a verb it usually appears in the passive, for example:

Please be seated.

583 Stationary and stationery

Wrong: The vehicle was stationery.
Correct: The vehicle was stationary.

'Stationary' means 'at rest'; 'stationery' means writing or office materials. (See number 25.)

584 Taken and taking

Wrong: We have not yet taking our breakfast.
Correct: We have not yet taken our breakfast.

See notes on numbers 553 and 580.

585 Taught and thought

Wrong: I taught Sati had gone; I was surprised to see him here.
Correct: I thought Sati had gone; I was surprised to see him here.

'Taught' is the Past Simple Tense of 'teach'; 'thought' is the Past Simple Tense of 'think'.

586 Their and there

Wrong: They collected there certificates.
Correct: They collected their certificates.

'There' is an adverb, 'their' a possessive; 'there' can never be used before a noun.

587 This and these

Wrong: Please put this books on the table.
Correct: Please put these books on the table.

'This' is singular; the 'i' is pronounced /ɪ/. 'These' is plural; the 'i' in the middle is pronounced /iː/.

588 Throne and thrown

Wrong: The present King came to the thrown in 1980.
Correct: The present King came to the throne in 1980.

'Thrown' is the Past Participle of 'throw'.

Now do Exercises 43 to 47.

12 Common Misspellings

Wrong spelling is often the result of confusing two words spelled similarly.

589 Argument

Wrong: arguement. *Correct:* argument.

The verb is 'argue', but the related noun has no -*e*- in the middle. In contrast, the verb 'judge' has a noun related to it ending in -*ment*, which can be spelled either 'judgement' or 'judgment'.

590 Christian

Wrong: Christain. *Correct:* Christian.

591 Convenient

Wrong: convinient. *Correct:* convenient.

592 Dining

Wrong: dinning. *Correct:* dining.

There is a verb 'dine', from which comes the word 'dining'. But the meal you take when you dine has double *n*: 'dinner'.

593 Grateful

Wrong: greatful. *Correct:* grateful.

Do not confuse this word with the adjective 'great'.

594 Grievous, grievances

Wrong: grievious, grieviances. *Correct:* grievous, grievances.

Note also: 'mischievous' (not: 'mischievious').

595 Hoping

Wrong: He was hopping to meet me at the airport, but I did not turn up.

Correct: He was hoping to meet me at the airport, but I did not turn up.

'Hoping' comes from 'hope', meaning 'expect'; 'hopping' comes from 'hop', meaning 'move on one leg only'.

596 In fact

Wrong: infact. *Correct:* in fact.

This is not one word like 'indeed'. 'In spite' must also be written as two words.

597 Length, strength

Wrong: lenght, strenght. *Correct:* length, strength.

These two words end in *-gth.* Note, however, that there are many words ending in *-ght:* 'height', 'ought', 'thought', 'taught', 'caught', 'bright', 'light', etc.

598 Maintenance

Wrong: maintainance. *Correct:* maintenance.

'Maintenance' is the noun derived from the verb 'maintain'.

599 Modern

Wrong: mordern. *Correct:* modern.

'Modern' sounds rather like 'northern', or it sounds as if the word 'order' were contained in it; but it has only one *r.*

600 Nonchalant

Wrong: nonchallant, non-challant. *Correct:* nonchalant.

The spelling of this word, meaning 'indifferent', must not be confused with 'challenge', or with many words that start with the prefix *non-,* such as 'non-fiction', 'non-stop', etc.

601 Occasion

Wrong: occassion. *Correct:* occasion.

Note other words that end in *-sion*; 'vision', 'division', 'fusion', 'confusion', 'invasion'.

Now note some words that do end in *-ssion*; 'passion', 'mission', 'fission', 'concussion'.

602 Prevalent

Wrong: prevailent. *Correct:* prevalent.

The verb is 'prevail', the adjective related to it, 'prevalent'.

603 Privilege

Wrong: priviledge. *Correct:* privilege.

Do not confuse this word with the many words that do end in *-dge*, such as 'judge', 'badge', 'lodge', etc.

604 Query

Wrong: querry. *Correct:* query.

Do not confuse 'query' with 'quarry' (a place from which stone is obtained), or with many other words that end in *-rry*, such as 'berry', 'merry', 'ferry', 'marry', 'worry'. Note also that 'bury' has only one *r*.

605 Strenuous

Wrong: strainous. *Correct:* strenuous.

'Strenuous' is the adjective derived from the noun 'strain'.

606 Super

Wrong: Since 1945 the world has been dominated by two supper-powers.

Correct: Since 1945 the world has been dominated by two super-powers.

'Supper' and 'super' are two quite different words. 'Supper' is a meal taken late in the day.

607 Until

Wrong: untill.   *Correct:* until.

'Until' and 'till' are two words having the same meaning, but 'until' has only one *l*.

Now do Exercise 48.

13 Words Mispronounced

English does not have a perfectly regular system of spelling. Many words are wrongly pronounced because the spelling suggests a certain pronunciation which is not correct. The following are common examples:

608 Architect
Do not pronounce the 'ch' like the 'ch' in 'church'. It is pronounced like 'k', as if the word were written 'arkitect'.

609 Available
The 'ai' here is pronounced like the 'a' of 'state', not like the 'a' of 'back'. The word should not be pronounced as if it were written 'avallable'.

610 Circuit
The 'uit' here is pronounced as if it were 'it'. Pronounce the word as if it were 'cirkit', not as if it were 'circute' or 'cirquit'.

611 Climb
Pronounce as if it were 'clime'; the 'b' is silent. Likewise, 'lamb' is pronounced as if it were 'lam', 'comb' as if it were 'coam', 'bomb' as if it were 'bom', and 'plumber' as if it were 'plummer'.

612 Debt
The 'b' is silent. Pronounce the word as if it were written 'dett'.

613 Elite
This word comes from French and still keeps a French type of pronunciation. It should sound like 'ay-leet' ('ay' as in 'day'), not like 'ee-light'.

614 Federal
The first 'e' is /e/, pronounced like 'e' in 'bed'. Pronounced in

the same way is the first 'e' in 'Senate'; also the 'ea' in 'weapon'. Do not let the words sound like 'fee-deral', 'See-nate', 'wee-pon'.

615 Gear
'G' at the beginning of a word is either 'soft' – pronounced like 'j', or 'hard' – pronounced like 'g' in 'get'. Before 'e' or 'i' it is usually soft, but there are a few words where it is hard, notably 'get', 'give', 'girl', and 'gear'. Do not let 'gear' sound like 'jeer'.

616 Hour
The 'h' is silent; 'hour' is pronounced in exactly the same way as 'our'. Other words with a silent 'h' include: 'honour', 'honest', 'honourable', and 'heir'. Likewise the letter 'h' is pronounced 'aitch', not 'haitch'.

617 Label
The 'a' is pronounced like the 'a' of 'state', not like the 'a' of 'back', as if the word were written 'labbel'. Likewise 'vacant' should be pronounced as if it were written 'vay-cant'.

618 Legal
The first three letters are not pronounced like the word *leg*. Say the word as if it started with 'lee'.

619 Lettuce
The 'u' here is like the 'i' of *is*; that is, /ɪ/. Say the word as if it were 'lettis'.

620 Listen
Pronounce as if it were 'lissen'. The 't' is silent. The 't' is silent also in *fasten*, *castle*, *bustle*.

621 Says
Do not model the pronunciation on that of 'say'. 'Says' is pronounced as if it were 'sezz'.

622 Shepherd
'Ph' is normally pronounced like 'f' in English, but this word is pronounced as if it were 'shepperd', not as if it were 'shefferd'; the 'h' is in fact silent.

623 Vehicle

The 'h' in the middle is silent. Pronounce the word as if it were 'vee-icle'.

624 Wednesday

Do not say 'Wed-nes-day'. The first 'd' is silent, and the word is pronounced as if it were 'Wensday'.

14 Errors of Punctuation

Punctuation means the use of printed signs other than letters, namely: full stops, colons, semicolons, commas, inverted commas, apostrophes, question and exclamation marks, hyphens, dashes, and brackets. The signs corresponding to these names are as follows:

full stop	.	apostrophe	'
colon	:	question mark	?
semicolon	;	exclamation mark	!
comma	,	hyphen	-
inverted commas	" "	dash	–
	' '	brackets	( )

Collectively these signs are known as punctuation marks. They are essential for dividing up written language into units that convey meaning. The wrong use of them, or failure to use them, will easily lead to misunderstanding. However, errors in punctuation are all too common, particularly where full stops, colons, semicolons and commas (the most frequently used punctuation marks) are concerned. To use these properly, it is necessary to be able to divide a sentence into the sub-units of meaning known as clauses: see pages 192–5. Further guidance on punctuation is given on pages 214–8.

625 Non-use of **full stop**

Wrong: The old woman carried the pile of wood home she had been working in the fields all day.

Correct: The old woman carried the pile of wood home. She had been working in the fields all day.

Wrong: The editor refused to publish my article he said it was inflammatory.

Correct: The editor refused to publish my article. He said it was inflammatory.

626 Wrong use of full stop: **although, though**

Wrong: 1 She said she wouldn't like a Toyota.
Though she later changed her mind.
2 She said she wouldn't like a Toyota.
Although she later changed her mind.

Correct: She said she wouldn't like a Toyota, though *or* although she later changed her mind.

'Though' or 'Although' introduces a subordinate clause in this example; therefore a comma, not a full stop, must come before. At the same time, note that 'though' (but not 'although') can be inserted into a sentence between commas, with the meaning 'however':

She said she wouldn't like a Toyota. Later, though, she changed her mind.

627 Wrong use of **full stop** before **thanks to**

Wrong: The building was completed in three months.
Thanks to the efforts of the villagers.

Correct: The building was completed in three months, thanks to the efforts of the villagers.

'Thanks to' is a preposition meaning simply 'because of', 'owing to', not a verb. The phrase introduced by 'thanks to' must therefore be part of a longer sentence.

628 Wrong use of **semicolon**

Wrong: When you have finished writing; I should like a word with you.

Correct: When you have finished writing, I should like a word with you.

'When you have finished writing' is a subordinate clause, and the only other clause in the sentence is the main clause, 'I should like a word with you'; therefore a semicolon cannot come between them.

629 Non-use of **comma**

Wrong: She went to the market and bought rice yams beans and fish.

Correct: She went to the market and bought rice, yams, beans, and fish.

Wrong: I had been feeling very sick and in any case I could not write to you because I had no money for writing-paper and envelopes.

Correct: I had been very sick, and in any case I could not write to you because I had no money for writing-paper and envelopes.

In the second example a comma needs to be put somewhere, and the ideal place is after 'sick' because 'I had been feeling sick' is one point, and separate from it is the fact that 'I could not write to you' together with the reason for this.

630 Wrong use of **inverted commas** (1)

Wrong: He said that 'it never rains but it pours'.

Correct: 1 He said that it never rains but it pours.
　　　　 2 'It never rains but it pours,' he said.

'He said that' introduces a statement in indirect speech, and no inverted commas are needed. A statement in direct speech, like the second correct example, needs inverted commas, but 'that' is omitted.

631 Wrong use of **inverted commas** (2)

Wrong: His name was 'John Smith'.

Correct: His name was John Smith.

Inverted commas are never used for a person's name or recognized title.

Wrong: Our boys won a 'resounding victory' over the opposing team.

Correct: Our boys won a 'resounding victory' over the opposing team, according to the Manager.

Inverted commas cannot be used to give prominence to some words in a sentence which the writer thinks important, like 'resounding victory'. They can and should be used, however, if the words they enclose represent the actual words used by somebody who is mentioned, such as the Manager in the second example. Inverted commas are also used to indicate the names of books, plays, etc. (see page 216.)

632 Wrong use of **apostrophe** (1)

Wrong: The dog caught it's leg in a trap.
Correct: The dog caught its leg in a trap.

It's (with apostrophe) is a contraction of *it is*. The possessive *its* (without apostrophe) is required here.

633 Wrong use of **apostrophe** (2)

Wrong: 'Am happy to tell you I've been accepted.
Correct: I'm happy to tell you I've been accepted.

The contraction of *I* and *am* is *I'm* (apostrophe between *I* and *m*). There is no such contraction as *'Am*.

In writing a hurried message, especially a telegram, one is looking for the briefest number of words possible, and then it is permissible to leave out pronouns altogether:

> Have just heard the news. Am on my way immediately.

This is not the same as a contraction using the apostrophe; and this type of omission must not be practised in formal writing, or even in friendly letters.

634 Wrong use of **dash**

Wrong: Askia Mohammed, who reigned from 1493–1528, was the greatest of Songhai's rulers.
Correct: 1 Askia Mohammed, who reigned from 1493 to 1528, was the greatest of Songhai's rulers.

2 Askia Mohammed (1493–1528) was the greatest of Songhai's rulers.

Now do Exercise 49.

15 Clichés

Clichés are expressions which to some ears may sound impressive, but to others have become tedious through overuse. They are not grammatically wrong, but they should be avoided by anyone who wishes to speak and write in a more individual and a more elegant way. In place of the cliché in question various alternative expressions can be found. Some suggestions are presented below, but they should not be regarded as the only suitable alternatives.

635 Does/did not augur well

Example: The breakdown of discipline which we are witnessing in schools does not augur well for the future of our country.

Alternatives: The breakdown of discipline which we are witnessing in schools is an ominous sign *or* is not a good sign for the future of our country.

636 Be that as it may

Example: The Government says that a lowering of the inflation rate is not feasible on economic grounds. Be that as it may, it is doubtful whether the present high level can be maintained.

'Be that as it may' has an unusual, quaint-sounding order of words that has become tedious to hear. Alternatives include 'That may be true, but . . .'; 'Whatever the case may be . . .'; 'However true that may be . . .'

637 The body politic

Example: Factionalism and sectionalism have troubled the body politic ever since the last election.

Alternatives: Factionalism and sectionalism have troubled the nation *or* the country *or* political life ever since the last election.

This is another tedious phrase, and one that is an exception to the rule that says that adjectives precede nouns in English; perhaps that accounts for its popularity.

638 Consequent upon this

Example: A new car loans policy was announced. Consequent upon this, the prices of cars rose dramatically.

Alternatives: A new car loans policy was announced. Consequently the prices of cars rose dramatically.

In general, do not use more words where fewer will serve just as well.

639 Dispense justice without fear or favour

Example: In his first address to the nation, the new President promised to dispense justice without fear or favour.

Alternatives: In his first address to the nation, the new President promised to dispense justice impartially *or* without partiality *or* fairly.

640 Finally and in conclusion

Example: Finally, and in conclusion, I will just say this – there is good reason to believe that the worst is over.

1 Finally, I will just say this – there is good reason to believe that the worst is over.
2 In conclusion, I will just say this – there is good reason to believe that the worst is over.

'Finally' and 'in conclusion' mean the same thing; so use one or the other but not both.

641 A force to be reckoned with
Example: Students have become a force to be reckoned with in national politics.
Alternatives: Students have become a major force *or* a powerful force *or* an important factor in national politics.

642 Last but not (the) least
Example: Last, but not least, I have the honour of introducing this night the Secretary-General of the National Union of Teachers.
Alternatives: Finally, *or* In conclusion, I have the honour of introducing this night the Secretary-General of the National Union of Teachers.

Everyone listening to the speaker is aware that somebody with a title as grand as Secretary-General of the National Union of Teachers is not 'the least' of those being introduced. To say 'not the least' is intended as a little joke, but it has nowadays come to seem very feeble.

643 Leave much to be desired
Example: The way he dealt with the bribery allegations left much to be desired.
Alternatives: The way he dealt with the bribery allegations was not very satisfactory.

This is just a long-winded way of condemning something or expressing disapproval of it.

644 Leave no stone unturned

Example: We should leave no stone unturned in our efforts to eliminate corruption and inefficiency.

Alternatives: We should make every effort to eliminate corruption and inefficiency.

645 To mention but a few

Example: Several important minerals are found in Central Africa: copper, cobalt, nickel, to mention but a few.

Alternatives: Several important minerals are found in Central Africa: copper, cobalt, nickel, and so on. *or* and many others. *or* etc. *or* for example.

646 The order of the day

Example: Immorality has become the order of the day in our society.

Alternatives: Immorality has become endemic *or* the rule *or* common practice in our society.

647 At that point in time

Example: Dr Doko assumed the directorship in 1978. At that point in time he had not yet been called to the Bar.

Instead of 'at that point in time', simply say 'at that time'.

648 Cannot/could not be overemphasized.

Example: The harm done to the good name of our institution cannot be overemphasized.

Alternatives: The harm done to the good name of our institution is enormous *or* colossal *or* indescribable.

649 No small measure

Example: Our advertising campaign will help in no small measure to improve the bad impression the public has of us.

Alternatives: Our advertising campaign will help greatly *or* enormously *or* immeasurably to improve the bad impression the public has of us.

650 The last straw that broke the camel's back

Example: The people had been accumulating grievances for many years before the rebellion started last June. The last straw that broke the camel's back was the Government's decision to quarter troops on their land.

This idiom is a homely, but wordy and an overused way of saying 'The final goad', 'The final irritation', 'The decisive provocation'. Or in the above example an alternative for the second sentence might be:

What finally pushed the people to revolt was the Government's decision to quarter troops on their land.

You are advised in conclusion to do Exercise 50. This is a general exercise covering all areas dealt with in the text.

16 Notes on Grammar

The purpose of this chapter is to give the learner a deeper understanding of some of the rules of English grammar, in the hope that this will strengthen his readiness to use correct forms and his resistance to incorrect forms. It does not seek to provide a comprehensive summary of English grammar, but concentrates on those aspects which need to be better understood if errors are to be avoided. First there is a section dealing with sentence structure as a whole. Then follows definitions and illustrations of selected topics of grammar. Finally, lists of various correct forms are given.

Readers seeking further guidance are advised to consult R A Close, *A Reference Grammar For Students of English* (Longman), or G Leech and J Svartvik, *A Communicative Grammar of English* (Longman).

I Sentence Structure

In using language we make sentences. If we do not make sentences our words lack meaning and we do not communicate. The following are sentences:

Obi kicked the ball.
Fatima, go to bed.
When he stood up, they all cheered.
I hear that you have done very well.

The following are not sentences:

Obi the ball.
go bed Fatima to
When he stood up,
That you have done very well.

There are four types of sentences, each communicating in a certain kind of way:

(a) Statements:
Obi kicked the ball.
She was busy washing dishes.
(b) Questions:
Did you write down my name?
Where will you spend the holiday?
(c) Commands:
Fatima, go to bed.
Take your papers to the Registrar.
(d) Exclamations:
How hot it is here!
What a lot of books you have!

The great majority of the sentences in a language, spoken or written, are statements.

Simple sentences

Sentences may be SIMPLE or they may be COMPLEX. Complex sentences may be broken up, or 'analyzed', into simple sentences; simple sentences can be combined into complex sentences.

Among sentences that function as statements, the simplest sentence consists of two words:

Audu spoke.
Dogs bark.
Clouds gathered.

The first of these words, the word on the left, is called the SUBJECT of the sentence; the other word is called the PREDICATE. The subject of a simple sentence is the person or thing about whom or about which something is said (*Audu, dogs, clouds*). The predicate is what is said about that person or thing (*spoke, bark, gathered*).

Most simple sentences consist of more than two words, but

in every sentence the same fundamental division can be made between subject and predicate:

SUBJECT	PREDICATE
The children	are playing.
The dam	was constructed in 1965.
My father's farm	is very extensive.
Audu	visited his mother last Friday.
All my friends	came.
She	bought a large quantity of rice.
A young man in glasses	stood up.

As the examples illustrate, there are many varieties of subject and predicate. In each of the sentences above, however, the subject is a NOUN PHRASE: in general a noun phrase must be the subject of a simple sentence. For further remarks on noun phrases, see page 195.

The predicate is more complicated:

1 It must contain a MAIN VERB (*spoke, bark,* etc.) which may be part of a VERB PHRASE employing an AUXILIARY VERB (*are playing; was constructed*; auxiliaries – *are, was*).
2 The verb or verb phrase may be followed by an OBJECT (*his mother* after *visited; a large quantity of rice* after *bought*).
3 The verb may be one that can be followed just by an ADJECTIVAL (*very extensive* after *is*).
4 The predicate may also include an ADVERBIAL (*in 1965; last Friday*).

The OBJECT of a verb is the person or thing affected by the action expressed by the verb. In a simple sentence the object of a verb is once again a noun phrase.

Some verbs may be followed by two objects (I gave *him a book*); some verbs are not followed by any object (*Audu has arrived*). A verb which can be followed by one or more objects is called TRANSITIVE; a verb which cannot be followed by an object is called INTRANSITIVE.

In simple sentences the position of an adverbial may be altered (*The dam was constructed in 1965* or *In 1965 the dam was constructed*). The position of all the other parts, and the order in which they come, is fixed; but also see 'Active and Passive' on page 205.

Summarizing, we can say that the structure of a simple sentence looks like this

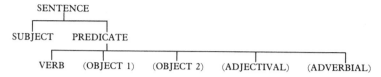

(Brackets indicate that the part in question need not be represented in the sentence.)

Complex sentences

Simple sentences can be joined together to make complex sentences. There are two ways of doing this: by CO-ORDINATION and by SUBORDINATION.

CO-ORDINATION means making use of one of these three conjunctions: *and, but, or*. For example:

1 Bisi entered the room. Bisi sat down. (Two simple sentences.)
   Bisi entered the room and (he) sat down. (One complex sentence.)
2 John handed over the money. The cashier did not give John a receipt. (Two simple sentences.)
   John handed over the money, but the cashier did not give him a receipt. (One complex sentence.)

Obviously, certain changes have to be made when sentences are combined: thus *Bisi* becomes *he, John* changes to *him*.

Each new complex sentence now consists of two CLAUSES, linked by a co-ordinating conjunction. Each of these clauses is a MAIN CLAUSE, which means that each is as important as the other in the total communication.

SUBORDINATION means joining two sentences together in such a way that the clauses which result are not of equal importance; one is made subordinate to the other. One is the MAIN CLAUSE:

the other is a SUBORDINATE CLAUSE. For example:

MAIN CLAUSE	SUBORDINATE CLAUSE
1 I spoke to Angela	who had just returned.
2 I enjoyed the meal,	though the meat was tough.
3 I am certain	that you will succeed.

Subordinate clauses may be FINITE or NON-FINITE. In finite clauses the verb phrase is one that could stand without change as the verb phrase of a simple sentence. For example, the first sentence above could be the result of combining the two simple sentences

I spoke to Angela. Angela had just returned.

The verb phrase in the simple sentence and the verb phrase in the subordinate clause of the complex sentence are identical (*had just returned*).

In a non-finite clause the verb phrase, if it is there at all, is one that would have to undergo some change in order to be the verb phrase of a simple sentence. For example:

I spoke to Angela, having just been introduced to her.
I spoke to Angela. I had just been introduced to her.

Here *having just been introduced to her* is a non-finite clause; the verb phrase in the sentence from which it is derived has a different form, *had been introduced*.

FINITE CLAUSES are of three broad types:
1 ADJECTIVAL (or 'RELATIVE'): linked usually to a noun or pronoun in the main clause, by a RELATIVE PRONOUN (*who, whom, whose, which, that*):

The boy *who greeted you* is my brother.
The medicine *which I bought yesterday* is finished.

2 NOMINAL (or NOUN CLAUSE): usually begins with *that*, or with a question word (*whether, who, what, which, where, how*, etc.). A noun clause functions like a noun phrase. For example:

1 *What you said* is very interesting. (Subject of *is*.)

2 I thought *(that) you were listening.* (Object of *thought.*)
3 It seems *(that) the fight is over.* (Complement of *seems.*)

A fourth type of clause is called 'appositive', meaning 'placed side by side', i.e. next to another noun:

4 I heard the rumour *that he had died.* (Apposite to *rumour.*)

3 ADVERBIAL: linked to the main clause by one of a variety of conjunctions, each giving a different meaning to the subordinate clause.

TIME *While you were eating,* I wrote a letter.
CONDITION: *If you don't stop crying,* I will beat you.
REASON: *Since it is raining now,* your plants will grow.
CONTRAST: *Although he likes volleyball,* he prefers athletics.
MANNER: He glared *as if I had just tried to rob him.*
RESULT: He was so humble *that everybody loved him.*
PURPOSE: I have come today *so that you can interview me at once.*
DEGREE: You eat more *than you realize.*

Like adverbials generally, adverbial clauses can often change position:

While you were eating, I wrote a letter.
I wrote a letter while you were eating.

NON-FINITE CLAUSES also of three broad types:
1 PARTICIPLE CLAUSES. (See page 205.) The verb in this type of clause is one word, ending in *-ing* or *-ed.* There may be a subject inside the clause, or it may lie outside the clause:

The visitors having left, we went to bed. (Subject: *the visitors.*)
Stunned by the news, I rushed to the gate. (Subject: *I.*)
Realizing his mistake, Ishola went away. (Subject: *Ishola.*)
2 INFINITIVE CLAUSES. (See page 205.) The verb is the infinitive, usually preceded by *to.* There may or may not be a subject in the clause:

To tell you the whole story will not be easy.
It will be hard *for her to forgive him.*

3 CLAUSES WITHOUT VERBS. These are usually quite short. It is possible to think of such a clause as an extract from a longer clause, through the omission of some part of the verb *be*:

You must set out tomorrow *if possible*.

Though my friend, he was not entirely honest.

A complex sentence may comprise several clauses, main or subordinate. For example:

It is clear that in recent years the balance of trade has not been in our favour, and if the economy of the country is going to improve we must seek to produce by ourselves many things which at present we import, however hard the task.

The structure of the sentence may be portrayed thus:

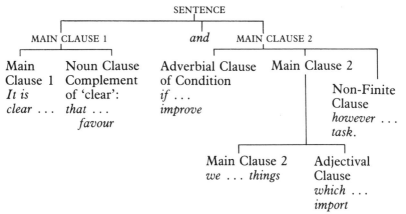

II Definitions and Illustrations

1 Noun phrases

A noun phrase can function as
(a) subject of a verb
(b) object of a verb
(c) complement of a linking verb
(d) object (or complement) of a preposition

The central element, sometimes the only element of a noun phrase, is a NOUN or a PRONOUN. In longer noun phrases the noun is preceded by one or more DETERMINERS, and preceded or followed by one or more ADJECTIVALS. Possible sequences therefore include:

Noun Phrase (here as Subject)		Predicate
NOUN	Audu	entered
PRONOUN	He	entered
DETERMINER + NOUN:	The doctor	entered
ADJECTIVAL + NOUN:	Old women	entered
DET + ADJ + NOUN:	A young doctor	entered
DET + ADJ + NOUN + ADJ:	A young man wearing a suit	entered
NOUN + ADJ:	Audu, who had just returned,	entered
DET + NOUN + ADJ:	The doctor, who had just returned,	entered

The structure of a noun phrase therefore looks like this:

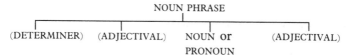

(Brackets indicate that the part in question need not be represented in the noun phrase.)

Note that the form of a pronoun changes when the pronoun is an object or comes after a preposition:

He asked for the money. I gave the money to *him*.

2 Adjectivals

As indicated in the previous section, some adjectivals are used *before* nouns, some are used *after* nouns. They fall into various types:

Adjectivals coming before nouns:
1 Several adjectives used together:

   fresh disturbing news; an *angry old* man: *clean white* socks.

2 Adjectives preceded by adverbs:

   very disturbing news; a *barely audible* voice; *brightly coloured* material.

3 Compound adjectives (two or more words linked by a hyphen):

   a *three-cornered* fight; *day-old* chicks; a *joint-stock* company.

Adjectivals coming after nouns:
1 Phrases beginning with a preposition:

   the peoples *of Africa*; the corner *of the room*; the clouds *in the sky*; the bridge *over the river*.

2 Phrases based on a participle:

   a book *belonging to my brother*; the houses *destroyed in the fire*; words *spoken in anger*; a job *well done*.

3 Finite Clauses (see page 193):
   The girl *who came to see you*; the rice *which he bought*; the bride-price *which he refused to pay*.

   Finite adjectival clauses are of two types, DEFINING and NON-DEFINING. A non-defining clause is one that makes a secondary point about the noun it goes with; if it were omitted the sentence would still have meaning. A non-defining clause is preceded by a comma. For example:

   Kola-nuts, *which have social uses in many parts of Africa*, are rather bitter in taste.
   Kola-nuts are rather bitter in taste.

In contrast, a defining clause could not be omitted:

A passport photograph must be attached. Anyone *who ignores this instruction* will be disqualified.

The second sentence would have no meaning here if it were simply *Anyone will be disqualified*. A defining clause is not preceded by a comma.

3 Countable and uncountable nouns

The majority of nouns are COUNTABLE. This means that they are names of things which exist as individual units with clear limits, and can therefore be counted. Common examples: *man, woman, house, farm, school, book, plate, cup, table, pen.* They can be used both in the singular and in the plural.

Many nouns on the other hand are UNCOUNTABLE, and their main feature is that they cannot be used in the plural, or with 'a' or 'an'. The mental picture which an uncountable noun presents, or should present, is that of a mass or substance or quality or concept with no well-defined limits, unless they are deliberately imposed. Common examples: *bread, rice, maize, milk, water, stationery, equipment, furniture, chalk, dust, air, information, advice, permission, courage, patience, happiness.*

Different sets of determiners are used before different types of nouns:

1 All nouns can be preceded by: *the*, possessives (*my*, etc.), *some, any, no, whose, which, what.*

2 Singular countable nouns can also be preceded by: *a (an), one, every, each, either, neither, this, that*, ordinal numbers (*first, second*, etc.), *another, next, last.*

3 Plural countable nouns can also be preceded by: *these, those*, cardinal numbers (*two, three*, etc.), *first, other, next, last, all, both, many, (a) few, several, more, enough.*

4 Uncountable nouns can also be preceded by: *this, that, much, (a) little, more, less, enough.*

Singular countable nouns cannot be used without a determiner, but plural countable nouns and uncountable nouns can be used without one:

He needs books.
He needs water.

It may seem strange to describe a word such as *money* as uncountable. The fact is that only *units* of money are countable, not money itself: hence we can say *five naira*, or *ten kwachas*, or *twenty shillings*, but not *five moneys*, etc. Thus to become countable something considered uncountable has to be mentally divided into units, and for a given uncountable noun there are certain suitable UNIT WORDS which can be used with it, and which are themselves countable. These words include *piece, item, bottle: a piece of (meat), an item of (equipment), a bottle of (beer)*.

Some nouns may be either countable or uncountable. For example: *salt* is uncountable when thought of as a mass of grains of salt used in cooking: *She bought some salt in the market*. But where different varieties are thought of, then the plural *salts* can be used:

Copper sulphate and ferrous oxide are commonly-occurring salts.

Lists of unit words and of nouns that can be both countable and uncountable appear on pages 220–22.

Note finally that in some books countable nouns are called COUNT NOUNS and uncountable nouns MASS NOUNS.

4 Use of articles

Note these general rules:

1 Either the indefinite article or the definite article must be used before singular countable nouns; a singular countable noun cannot be used without an article. For example:

The book lay on the table.
A book lay on the table.

It would never be correct to say *Book lay on the table*.

2 The indefinite article cannot be used before plural countable nouns or before uncountable nouns (*a books, a water* are not

correct); but the definite article can be used before either type of noun (*the books, the water*), and either can appear without an article (*books, water*).

These rules can be summarized in table form thus:

	DEFINITE ARTICLE	INDEFINITE ARTICLE	NO ARTICLE
SINGULAR COUNTABLE Nouns	Yes	Yes	No
PLURAL COUNTABLE Nouns	Yes	No	Yes
UNCOUNTABLE Nouns	Yes	No	Yes

Thus for singular countable nouns the choice lies between using the indefinite article or the definite article; for plural countable nouns and uncountable nouns the choice lies between using the definite article or no article. Further rules for taking the one available option or the other in each case can now be given.

Definite and Indefinite Reference

The use of *a* or *an* before singular countable nouns and the absence of any article before plural countable nouns and uncountable nouns indicates INDEFINITE REFERENCE. Reference is indefinite when something not previously known or not previously talked about is introduced in a sentence:

An exhibition of painting was held on Foundation Day.
Programmes were handed to guests at the door.
Water is now flowing through the pipes again.

The use of *the* before all types of nouns indicates DEFINITE REFERENCE. Reference is definite in the following circumstances.

1 When mention is made of something already referred to:

An exhibition of painting was held on Foundation day. Several well-known artists took part. *The exhibition* was followed by speeches in our main hall.

200

2 When only one thing or group of things indicated by the noun exists in a given situation, or the noun indicates an institution or an experience familiar to everybody:

The President has arrived.
He died during *the War*.
Please turn on *the radio*.
She was busy in *the kitchen*.

No previous mention needs to be made of, say, 'President', because it is recognized that 'the President' means 'the President of our country'. 'A President' would mean the President of a different country, not ours.

3 Something may be made definite when an adjectival such as a *wh*-clause or a prepositional phrase is added to the noun:

The causes *of the drought* are being studied.
The sugar *which you bought* yesterday has disappeared.

However, definiteness does not necessarily result when an adjectival is added:

Information which we have just received confirms that he was shot.

Specific and Generic Reference

Reference is said to be SPECIFIC when a noun refers to one or several objects in a set, and GENERIC when a noun refers to all objects in a set: for example, *books* may mean all possible books, all books ever written (*generic*), or only some among those that have been written or could be written (*specific*). The meaning dictates the choice of article, according to the type of noun used.

Countable Nouns:
Both specific and generic reference can be indicated by the use of the indefinite article (before single countable nouns) or its omission (before plural countable nouns), or by the use of *the*:
1 A man was coming towards us. (One man: specific.)
2 A man ought to be proud of his children. (All men: generic.)

3 Men ⎱ were coming towards us. (Some men: specific.)
  Some men ⎰
4 Men ought to be proud of their children. (All men: generic.)
5 The python moved slowly through the grass. (One python: specific.)
6 The python is sacred in their culture. (Any kind of python: generic.)
7 The pythons were slaughtered. (Several: specific.)

Uncountable Nouns:
Both specific and generic reference can be indicated by the omission of the definite article (the indefinite article can never be used before uncountable nouns in any case):

Water is necessary for life. (Generic.)
Water is flowing through the pipes at last. (Specific.)

The use of *the* gives specific reference when an adjectival is also used after the noun:

The water *in this tank* seems stagnant.
(Omission of *the* here would be wrong.)

Sometimes it is debatable whether the reference of a noun having an adjectival in front of or after it is specific or generic. This is a matter for linguists; the important thing for the learner is to know when to use *the*. A fairly reliable rule, for abstract nouns at least, states that when an adjectival comes before the noun *the* is omitted; but when it is used in an *of*-phrase coming after the noun, *the* is necessary:

ABSTRACT NOUN	ADJECTIVAL BEFORE NOUN	ADJECTIVAL AFTER NOUN
physics	Newtonian physics	the physics of Newton
geography	West African geography	the geography of West Africa
theology	Christian theology	the theology of Christianity
metabolism	plant metabolism	the metabolism of plants

5 Order of determiners

See the list of determiners on page 39, and the rules for their

use with different types of nouns set out on pages 198–9.
This table gives guidance for the proper *ordering* of determiners
in relation to one another:

1	2	3
amount words: all, both, half, twice, three times, one-third, etc.	the, a, an *possessives*: my, your, his, etc. *demonstratives*: this, that, these, those; nouns in -'s *amount words*: some, any, no, every, each, much	*cardinal numbers*: one, two, etc. *ordinal numbers*: first, second, etc. *amount words*: many, few, little, several, more, less next, last, other

Possible sequences according to the table include:
column 1 + (adjective +) noun: *all (honest) men*, etc.
          1 + 2 + noun: *all my books, both those houses, half the money*, etc.
          1 + 2 + 3 + noun: *all his other friends*, etc.
          2 + noun: *this book, Eze's hat, some students*, etc.
          2 + 3 + noun: *the first tree, a few teeth*, etc.
          3 + noun: *two goats, more food*, etc.
Forbidden sequences include, in general,
(i) two (or more) determiners from the same column, e.g. *all* and *both*, *this* and *my*, *no* and *any*;
(ii) two amount words, e.g. *all* and *some*, *any* and *several*, etc.; but *some, any* can precede *few*; and see rules for *much, more,* and *other* which follow.
Special notes:
1 MORE can *only* be used after: *some, any, no, many, few, little, several* and cardinal numbers. This applies to *more* as an amount word, not to *more* indicating degree, which can be used after other determiners, e.g.:

I have never seen a more beautiful woman.

2 MUCH can *only* be used after *this* or *that* or before *more, less, other*.

3 OTHER can be used before or after column 3 words, but it must follow and not be preceded by *many, few, little, several,* and cannot be used with *more. An* followed by *other* becomes one word, *another.*

4 NEXT and LAST can be used before or after cardinals (*next two, two next,* etc.) and after *the,* possessives, demonstratives, nouns in *-'s;* but not with amount words or ordinals.

5 Other determiners not listed are: (*a*) *certain, enough, which . . .? what . . .?* They must be used directly before adjectives or nouns, but *other* can be used after them: *enough fuel, which country?, certain other people,* etc.

6 Many of the determiners listed can be followed by *of* and then by *the,* possessives, demonstratives, and nouns in the plural, creating possibilities of many fresh sequences: *all of the rooms, many of our townspeople, which of the chairs?* etc. *Either* and *neither* can be used in the same way: *either of those wheels, neither of my parents.*

6 Verb phrases

1 TENSES: *give* is used as an example.

	ACTIVE	PASSIVE
Present Simple	I give	I am given
Present Continuous	I am giving	I am being given
Past Simple	I gave	I was given
Past Continuous	I was giving	I was being given
Present Perfect Simple	I have given	I have been given
Present Perfect Continuous	I have been giving	–
Past Perfect Simple	I had given	I had been given
Past Perfect Continuous	I had been giving	–

Each tense is shown as formed with *I* as subject, but there are certain variations with other pronoun subjects. With *he, she, it,* and singular (including uncountable) nouns, the present simple is *gives. I am* becomes *you are, he is, she is, it is, we are, they are; I was* becomes *we were, you were, they were; I have* becomes *he has, she has, it has*, etc.

The designations of the personal pronouns are as follows:

I: 1st person singular
we: 1st person plural
you: 2nd person singular *or* plural
he, she, it: 3rd person singular
they: 3rd person plural

2 *Infinitives and Participles*

	ACTIVE	PASSIVE
Present Simple Infinitive	to give	to be given
Present Continuous Infinitive	to be giving	–
Perfect Simple Infinitive	to have given	to have been given
Perfect Continuous Infinitive	to have been giving	–
Present Participle	giving	being given
Perfect Participle	having given	having been given
Past Participle	given	–

3 *Auxiliaries*

Auxiliary verbs are used before the various infinitives, producing six possible phrases for each auxiliary. Those with *shall* and *will* are sometimes called FUTURE tenses, those with *should* and *would* CONDITIONAL tenses, for example:

will {
give
be giving
have given
have been giving
be given
have been given
}

should {
give
be giving
have given
have been giving
be given
have been given
}

7 *Active and passive*

See the remarks against numbers 216 and 217 and also the table of tenses on page 204. This table should make it clear that for every ACTIVE tense, infinitive, and participle there is a corresponding PASSIVE tense, infinitive, or participle. This is true, however, only for verbs that can take an object, i.e. transitive verbs. Intransitive verbs (*go, come, arrive, remain, fall, die*, etc.) have no passive forms: it is impossible to say *is being gone, had been arrived*, etc.

Active sentences (sentences where the main clause verb is active) can usually be transformed into passive sentences:

1(a) Philip drank the beer. (Active.)
 (b) The beer was drunk by Philip. (Passive.)
2(a) The small boy is guiding the cows to the river. (Active.)
 (b) The cows are being guided to the river by the small boy. (Passive.)

When two sentences are related like 1a and 1b or 2a and 2b, the object of the active sentence becomes the subject of the passive sentence; while the subject of the active sentence is put after *by* in a prepositional phrase, and is called the AGENT.

In very many passive sentences, however, the agent is omitted. The focus of attention may be on the subject and what happens to the subject; mention of the agent is needless or irrelevant. For example:

The new forms have not yet been issued.
Efforts will be made to retrieve the stolen goods.

This is called the 'impersonal' passive, and it is widely used in academic and administrative English.

Passive infinitives and participles are also common:

I do not wish *to be caught*.
After *being examined* by the doctor, you will go for a blood test.

8 Use of continuous forms

The table on page 204 shows that a verb has a maximum of eight active tenses, of which four are simple and four continuous, and six passive tenses, of which four are simple and two continuous. There are many verbs, however, which have simple tenses only, or if they do have continuous forms these are not often used: e.g., it is possible to say *I know* but not *I am knowing; it equals* but not *it is equalling*.

The reason for this deficiency is that a continuous form expresses a process or a regular or repeated event. The meaning of *know* or *equal*, in contrast, can only be thought of as a state or condition; no meaning can be given to *I am knowing* or *it is equalling*.

While there is a small number of verbs of which it can safely be said that they have no continuous forms, there are many others whose continuous forms are rarely used or used much less frequently than the simple forms. Common verbs in each group are as follows:

1 No Continuous Forms:
   belong to, concern, comprise, consist of, contain, deserve, equal, have (meaning 'possess'), *matter, own, possess, resemble, seem, suffice.*

2 Continuous Forms Rarely Used:
   believe, cost, depend on, desire, doubt, fit, forget, forgive, hate, hear, imagine, intend, know, like, love, mean, need, perceive, please, prefer, realize, recognize, remember, require, satisfy, see, suppress, understand, want.

Certain verbs in addition are quite commonly used with two meanings, for one of which the continuous forms may be used, but not for the other:

1(a) These eggs smell bad. (They give off a bad smell.)
 (b) He was smelling the meat. (He was exercising his sense of smell.)

2(a) It appears you are rich. (It seems . . .)
 (b) The moon is appearing from behind the clouds. (It is coming into view.)

9 Linking verbs

In the sentence *Matthew is my friend* there is identity between *Matthew* and *my friend*; in the sentence *Matthew saw my friend* there is no identity between *Matthew* and *my friend*. In the sentences *Joseph feels happy* and *Joseph seems sad*, *happy* and *sad* are adjectives describing Joseph, even though in each case noun and adjective are separated by a verb.

When the subject of a sentence is connected in this way to a noun phrase or an adjectival and the two are separated by a main verb, the verb is called a LINKING VERB. The most common linking verb is *be* (in all its forms); others are *seem, look, appear, feel, sound, become, taste, turn, grow, fall*. Some of these also function as ordinary verbs with an object:

(a) We tasted the stew.
(b) The stew tasted good.

Only in (b) is *taste* a linking verb.

10 Complements

A complement means the word or words needed after linking verbs and after certain adjectives and nouns to give them complete meaning; for example, *Chinwe seems* has no meaning unless something follows *seems: very clever, a sweet girl, to have left, in difficulty*, etc. Each of these when following *seems* is called a complement of *seems*.

As these examples indicate, complements are of various types:

(a) noun phrase: *a sweet girl*
(b) adjectival: *very clever*
(c) prepositional phrase: *in difficulty*
(d) *to* + verb: *to have left*
(e) *that*-clause: It seems *that Chinwe has left.*
(f) adverb: The match seems *over.*

Complements of various types are found after

1 Linking Verbs. (See above.)
2 Adjectives, as in

I am happy *that you have found him.*
She will be glad *to see you.*
You are good *at mathematics.*

3 Nouns, as in

They considered Patrick *a genius.*
He considers driving *dangerous.*

11 Sequence of tenses

This section should be read together with the general advice given on pages 79–80.
Now look at the following tables.

I Statements about PRESENT time:

| Yusuf claims that he | knows the President, doesn't eat meat, once owned a car, didn't go to primary school, is a police officer, was born in 1910, has been to America, will soon be made a chief, may one day marry again, | but | I don't believe him. few people are convinced. who $\begin{Bmatrix} \text{will} \\ \text{can} \end{Bmatrix}$ believe him? |

II Statements about PAST time:

| My late uncle claimed that he | knew the President, didn't eat meat, had once owned a car, hadn't gone to primary school, was a police officer, had been to America, would soon be made a chief, might one day marry again, | but | I didn't believe him. few people were convinced. who $\begin{Bmatrix} \text{would} \\ \text{could} \end{Bmatrix}$ believe him? |

In Table I, statements are made about Yusuf in the present, e.g.: *Yusuf claims that he once owned a car, but who will believe him?* Each possible sentence is complex, consisting of a main clause (*Yusuf claims . . .*); an object clause (*that he once owned a car*); and a co-ordinated main clause (*but who will believe him?*). Because the tense of the main clause is present, the tenses in all the other clauses must either be present tenses (where what he claims is supposed to be true in the present) or past tenses (where what he claims is supposed to have been true in the past).

In Table II, similar statements are made about 'my late uncle', but this time his claims are past claims, e.g.: *My late uncle claimed that he didn't eat meat, but who could believe him?* This time the tenses used in the subordinate clauses must be past tenses if they were present tenses in Table I, and must be in the past perfect if they were past tenses in Table 1. Comparing both tables we observe these changes of tense:

I		II
present	→	past
past	→	past perfect

In more detail: *knows* changes to *knew*, *don't believe* to *didn't believe*, *doesn't eat* to *didn't eat*, *is* to *was*, *are* to *were*, *has* to *had*, *will* to *would*, *can* to *could*, *may* to *might*, *owned* to *had owned*.

12 Participles

Each verb has two participles, one ending in *-ing* ('present participle'), the other ending in *-ed* ('past participle'; some irregular verbs have other past participle endings).

The principal use of participles is in the formation of tenses. However, they are extremely useful in certain other ways also:

1 *Verb-Nouns.* The *-ing* participle can function just like a noun:

(a) as subject of a verb: *Smoking is bad for health.*

(b) as object of a verb: *He detests smoking.*

(c) preceded by determiners: *The singing has stopped.*

(d) preceded by prepositions: *He was against dancing.*

While functioning as nouns, however, participles may keep the characteristics of verbs. Objects can follow them:

He likes taking *snuff*.
He was praised for saving *his friend's life*.

The *-ing* participle used as a verb-noun may or may not be used in the plural with *-s*. Some examples are given on page 227.

2 *Verb-Adjectives.* Both the *-ing* participle and the *-ed* participle can function as adjectives. As verb-adjectives they are essential to the formation of the principal types of non-finite clauses, described on pages 194–5.

13 Direct and indirect speech

Ability to operate the sequence of tenses rule, which has been outlined in section 12, is essential to making statements and questions in indirect speech and in converting direct to indirect speech.

Look at these four sentences:

1(a) 'I can speak many languages,' says Yusuf.
(*Or*: 'I can speak many languages,' Yusuf says.)
(b) Yusuf says he can speak many languages.
2(a) 'I can speak many languages,' said Yusuf.
(b) Yusuf said he could speak many languages.

In 1a and 2a the actual words of Yusuf are being directly quoted; the words *says Yusuf* and *said Yusuf*, which lie outside the quotation marks, are merely those of the writer and are introduced to let the reader know who spoke the words within the quotation marks. 'I can speak many languages' is an example of DIRECT SPEECH in this context.

In 1b and 2b, in contrast, the actual words of Yusuf are not quoted. The writer reports Yusuf's statement, but because after *says* or *said* the next word used is *that*, the Sequence of Tenses rule comes into operation, and in 2b we find *could* instead of *can*. Another change is that *I* changes to *he*. Thus Yusuf's words are no longer being directly quoted; and 1b and 2b are examples of INDIRECT SPEECH.

All the four sentences above are statements, because the verb *say* is used. 1a and 2a present Yusuf's words as a DIRECT STATE-MENT, while 1b and 2b present what he has said as a REPORTED or INDIRECT STATEMENT. Other verbs used to indicate statements are: *announce, add, argue, declare, maintain*, etc. In the writer's 'presentation' of the direct statement, verb can be inverted with subject: *says Yusuf* or *Yusuf says, added Yusuf* or *Yusuf added*, etc.

Now look at these sentences:

3(a) 'Is it raining?' asks Mary.

(b) Mary asks if *or* whether it is raining.

4(a) 'Is it raining?' asked Mary.

(b) Mary asked if *or* whether it was raining.

Here we have DIRECT QUESTIONS (3a, 4a) and INDIRECT QUESTIONS (3b, 4b), and the same rules apply as to direct and indirect statements. But the rules for converting direct question forms into indirect question forms are rather more complicated. Note, first, that in direct questions subject and verb are inverted, and that when no *wh*-word (*who, what*, etc.) comes at the beginning of the question, *if* or *whether* must be introduced in the indirect question form. Then observe what happens to a direct question beginning with a part of *do* when converted into an indirect question:

5(a)'Does it often rain?' asks Mary.

(b) Mary asks whether it often rains.

6(a) 'Does it often rain?' asked Mary.

(b) Mary asked whether it often rained.

A *wh*-word used in a direct question is retained in the indirect form:

7(a) 'When was the road constructed?' he asked.

(b) He asked when the road was constructed.

Other verbs indicating questions besides *ask* are *inquire* and *wonder*.

There are various other complications in converting direct to indirect speech, such as pronoun changes. Lack of space prevents attention to the details here, but common sense should suggest why such changes are made in these sentences:

8(a) 'James, why have you disappointed us?' he asked.

(b) He asked James why he had disappointed them.

9(a) 'We are happy to see you,' they said.

(b) They said they were happy to see him *or* her *or* them.

14 Word classes

The words of English fall into the following classes:

1 *Major Word Classes*:

MAIN VERBS   *go, see, write, leave, get, find*, etc.
NOUNS   *Peter, woman, river, truth, Africa*, etc.
ADJECTIVES   *good, old, black, useful, different*, etc.
ADVERBS   *slowly, probably, now, there, very*, etc.

2 *Minor Word Classes*:

DETERMINERS   *the, a (an), some, this, my*, etc.
PRONOUNS   *he, it, us, everyone, nothing, themselves*, etc.
AUXILIARY VERBS   *do, can, will, may, used to*, etc.
PREPOSITIONS   *in, on, at, by, with, for*, etc.
CONJUNCTIONS   *and, but, or, if, although*, etc.
INTERJECTIONS   *oh!*, etc.

The distinction between MAJOR and MINOR word classes is chiefly that the major word classes contain the great majority of the words of English, and each major class is capable of growth through the addition of new words; while the minor word-classes contain relatively few words and fresh words are rarely added to any class. Nevertheless all classes, with the exception of interjections, are important in building up sentences.

It is essential for the learner to know which class an individual word falls into, and how words in that class behave. Guidance is given on this at the head of the relevant chapter earlier in the book. At the same time, very many words can function in more than one class. Here are common examples:

play: (a) They are going to play football. (Verb)
    (b) We saw a play last night. (Noun)
back: (a) She has injured her back. (Noun)
    (b) If you back me, we can succeed. (Verb)
    (c) He threw the ball back. (Adverb)

	(d) You can sit on the back seat. (Noun as Adjective)
state:	(a) Please state your objection. (Verb)
	(b) They were in a state of confusion. (Noun)
	(c) Apply to the State Government. (Noun as Adjective)
right:	(a) You have no right to do that. (Noun)
	(b) Now I know you were right. (Adjective)
	(c) He sought to right many wrongs. (Verb)
	(d) Things will never go right for you. (Adverb)
major	(a) He lives near a major road. (Adjective)
	(b) He is a Major in the Army. (Noun)
	(c) She majored in chemistry. (Verb)
second	(a) He came second in the test. (Adjective)
	(b) You are ten seconds too late. (Noun)
	(c) Who will second the motion? (Verb)

15 Punctuation marks

Here are a few guidelines for the use of punctuation marks:

Full stop
A full stop indicates a pause, and marks off one sentence from another. After a full stop a new sentence must begin with a capital letter.

Semicolon
A semicolon also indicates a pause, but a shorter one than a full stop. A semicolon separates one complete statement from another, and the second statement does not have to be introduced by 'and' or 'but'. This is a good way of linking statements when they are part of the same trend of thought:

He left the house at 7 o'clock; he did not return until 4.

The ambitious learner of English (and other languages) will seek to develop the use of semicolons. They give an impression of someone who can recognize connections between ideas and organize his thoughts.

Another use of semicolons is in listing items when a comma,

which is the natural punctuation mark for lists, is needed for other purposes:

Those attending the ceremony included His Highness Chief Adekunle II, the Oba of Ogboland; the Chairman of New Africa Bank, Ltd., Alhaji Mohammed Toro; and the Managing Director of Platco Products (Ltd.), Mr. Joseph Odili.

Colon

A colon has the same weight as a semicolon, i.e. it is not so strong a pause as a fullstop. It serves mainly to introduce or present a point or item that follows on from what has been said before:

We all know the reasons for his flight: he was under investigation for fraud.

Comma

A comma indicates a pause, but is less strong than even a semicolon or colon. Rules for the use of commas are not easy to give, but note:

1 Commas are used to mark off items in a list, including lists of facts:

I disliked his greed, his boastfulness, and his lack of manners.

2 Commas must not be used before noun clauses (see page 193) and defining clauses (see page 197).
3 Commas are used to mark off non-defining clauses (see page 197), participle clauses and verbless clauses (see page 195), and sentence adverbs:

Mauritania, which adjoins Senegal, is mainly desert.
I left at once, shocked by his indifference.
You are advised, if in difficulties, to go on to the next question.
It was observed, however, that no reply was given.

4 There is much greater freedom in the use of commas before or after adverbial clauses. Where there is just one adverbial

clause in a sentence and it is the only subordinate clause there, the comma can be used or it can be omitted:

When I saw you I did not at first recognize you.
When I saw you, I did not at first recognize you.

In longer sentences commas must be used, but with discretion. They must certainly not be over-used. A sentence punctuated like this would be ridiculous:

Although he said he had been reading throughout the night, I knew that this was a lie, because there was no light coming from his room, when I passed by.

But this too would be unsatisfactory:

Although he said he had been reading throughout the night I knew that this was a lie because there was no light coming from his room when I passed by.

A comma needs to be used in at least one place, and the best place would be after the *Although*-clause because the point stated there stands rather apart from the other points of the sentence, which themselves form a closer group. So the best punctuation of the sentence would be:

Although he said he had been reading throughout the night, I knew that this was a lie because there was no light coming from his room when I passed by.

Inverted commas.
These go in pairs, and they can be either double or single:

"What is your name?" *or* 'What is your name?'

Single inverted commas are more fashionable nowadays.

Inverted commas are used (1) to indicate direct speech, i.e. to distinguish somebody's words quoted by the writer from the writer's own statements:

'What is your name,'   Olu asked.
———————————   ———————————
Olu's quoted words   writer's statement

Inverted commas are also used (2) to indicate titles of books, plays, newspapers, magazines, etc. They are *not* used for names and titles of people unless these are nicknames:

Mr Otaro was known as 'Bulldozer'.

Apostrophe.
An apostrophe resembles the second in a pair of single inverted commas. It is used to indicate possession: e.g. *the boy's father, the students' rooms*. Note these points:
  i If the possessor is a singular noun, the noun is followed by an apostrophe and then *s*: *the boy's father*.
  ii If the possessor is a plural noun which already ends in *-s*, only an apostrophe is added: *the students' rooms*.
  iii If the possessor is a personal name already ending in *-s*, an apostrophe and then *s* are added: *James's brother*.
An apostrophe also indicates the absence of a letter in contractions such as *isn't* (for *is not*), *he's* (for *he is*), *they're* (for *they are*), *I'd* (for *I had* or *I should* or *I would*), *she'll* (for *she will*), etc.

Question mark, exclamation mark.
As the names indicate these mark questions and exclamations respectively. They are needed and are widely used in direct speech and personal letters, but they are inappropriate and should be avoided in indirect speech and formal writing, such as essays and compositions.

Brackets.
These mark off words which the writer considers incidental to what has gone before, and so less important:

Martin was planning (nobody knew why) to sell off the beautiful equipment he had taken so much trouble to acquire.

Brackets do *not* indicate words that should be ignored entirely; they should not be used when the writer makes a mistake and wants to delete the words. Instead, a line should be put through the words.

Dashes.

A pair of dashes functions like a pair of brackets:

> Martin was planning – nobody knew why – to sell off the beautiful equipment he had taken so much trouble to acquire.

A single dash is used to indicate words added as an afterthought:

> William finally married Elizabeth – the woman he had always loved.

On the whole brackets and dashes should be avoided, and where possible commas should be used instead.

Hyphen.

A hyphen looks like a short dash, and must be written in such a way as to bind two words closely together (*oil-field*, not *oil - field*). This indicates its function in grammar, which is to join two words together to form a compound, e.g. *oil-field*, *air-conditioner*, *radio-cassette*, *self-conscious*.

Many words, however, are joined together to form a true compound with no hyphen (*rainfall, passport, newspaper*), while in other cases two words are used together but are kept separate and no hyphen is used (*air letter, postage stamp, greetings card*). A good dictionary will show when a hyphen must be used.

III Lists of Correct Forms

1 Nouns: singulars and plurals

The general rule for forming the plural of a singular noun is; add *-s*. Exceptions:
1 Nouns ending in *-s* already, or in *-ch, -sh, -x*; add *-es*. For example: *gas, gases; watch, watches; bush, bushes; box, boxes.*
2 Nouns ending in *-y* change the *-y* to *-i*, then add *-es*:
lady, ladies; ferry, ferries; duty, duties.
But nouns ending in *-ay, -ey, -oy, -uy* obey the general rule and add *-s*:
day, days; monkey, monkeys; boy, boys; guy, guys.

3 Nouns ending in *-f* or *-fe*:
   (a) the following change *-f* to *v* before adding *-es*:
      leaf, life, half, loaf, calf, knife, wife, thief, shelf, scarf,
      Plurals: *leaves, lives, halves,* etc.
   (b) The rest add *-s* in the usual way: *chief, chiefs; roof, roofs,*
      etc.
4 Nouns ending in *-o*:
   (a) some add *-es*: *tomato, tomatoes; potato, potatoes; mango,*
      mangoes, likewise *cargo, hero, veto, echo.*
   (b) the rest add *-s*: *piano, pianos; kilo, kilos, etc.*
5 Irregular plurals:
   man, men; woman, women; child, children; ox, oxen; sheep,
   sheep; foot, feet; tooth, teeth, and a few others.
6 Foreign plurals: nouns ending in *-us, -is, -ix, -a, -um,*
   -on. These are words brought into English from Greek or
   Latin, which often still keep the plural endings of these
   languages:
   -us: *bonus, bonuses; campus, campuses; chorus, choruses;* but:
         focus, focuses or *foci; nucleus, nucleuses* or *nuclei; radius,*
         radiuses or *radii; syllabus, syllabuses* or *syllabi; stimulus,*
         stimuli.
   -is: *basis, bases; crisis, crises.* Likewise: *oasis, thesis, hypoth-*
         esis, analysis, diagnosis.
   -ix: *appendix, appendices.*
   -a: *area, areas; idea, ideas;* but: *formula, formulas* or
         formulae.
   -um: *album, albums; museum, museums; stadium, stadiums;*
         but *curriculum, curricula; medium, media* ('the mass
         media'); *memorandum, memorandums* or *memoranda.*
         Data, a plural noun, normally has no singular form.
   -on: *electron, electrons; demon, demons;* but *criterion, criteria.*
7 Plural noun, no singular form:
   (a) *cattle, police, people* (meaning 'human beings', no matter
      the race);
   (b) nouns ending in *-s* referring to two equal parts together:
      glasses (meaning 'spectacles'), *pants, pyjamas, scales*
      (meaning 'a balance for weighing'), *scissors, shorts*
      (meaning 'short trousers'), *trousers;*

(c) other nouns ending in -*s*:

amends (in *make amends*), *arrears* (in *be in arrears*), *auspices* (*under the auspices of*), *clothes*, *funds* (meaning 'money in general'), *goods* (meaning 'property', 'freight', as in *goods train*), *looks* (in *good looks*, meaning 'attractive appearance'), *manners* (*bad manners*, meaning 'bad social behaviour'), *minutes* (meaning 'record of a meeting'), *outskirts* (fringes of a town), *pains* (in *take pains*), *remains* (meaning 'remaining part' of something dead or destroyed), *quarters* (meaning 'dwelling-place'), *regards* (in *send my regards*, *give my regards*).

8 Nouns ending in -*s*, but treated as singular:

news; and names of branches of study: *economics, mathematics, physics, statistics*, etc.

2 Uncountable nouns

The nouns listed are a selection of everyday words, not a complete list.

1 Nouns which are always uncountable:

(a) concrete: *bread, butter, milk, rice, steam, smoke, moisture, dust, rubbish, chalk, flesh, gold, copper, oxygen*, etc.

(b) abstract: *adolescence, agriculture, behaviour, bravery, capitalism, destruction, electricity, erosion, extravagance, furniture, honesty, hunger, hygiene, independence, information, knowledge, magic, music, news, patience, peace, photography, poetry, poultry, publicity, retirement, sunshine, taxation, violence, wealth*, etc.

Also in this category are medical names for illnesses: *malaria, hepatitis* (and all words ending in -*itis*), *yellow fever, jaundice, billharzia, leprosy, pneumonia, kwashiorkor, rickets, cancer, catarrh, gonorrhoea, eczema*, etc.

Another group is the names of branches of study (but also see below): *archaeology, geography, mathematics, medicine*, etc.

2 Nouns which are generally uncountable, but may be countable when *different types* are being considered:

(a) concrete: *beer, food, liquid, paint, sand, soil, soap, sugar, wood*, etc.

(b) abstract: *disease, fever, history, industry, money, philosophy, pleasure, science, stationery, style.*

3 Nouns with two meanings, one as a countable, the other as an uncountable noun:
cold, competition, conflict, drink, law, light, order, position, power, production, scholarship, sense, space, speech, stone, war, weight, etc. Such nouns are quite numerous. Examples:

1(a) He has lost the faculty of speech. (Uncountable)
 (b) Many speeches were made in favour of the plan. (Countable)
2(a) The statue is made of stone. (Uncountable)
 (b) The children pelted the dog with stones. (Countable)
3(a) We believe in the rule of law. (Uncountable)
 (b) The laws of any country can be changed. (Countable)

4 Nouns generally uncountable, but occasionally used in the plural:
air (but *give oneself airs,* meaning 'boast'); *blood*; *water* (but *the waters of the Nile*).

3 Unit Nouns, Group Nouns

1 Common unit words used before uncountable nouns include:
 (a) general words: *piece, item, lump, grain, slice, drop, block,* etc.
 (b) containers: *cup, bottle, packet, tin,* etc.
 (c) measures: *litre, kilo,* etc.
 (d) 'type' words: *type, kind, sort, brand,* etc.
 Unit words indicating containers, measures, and types can also be used with countable nouns.
 Examples: *a piece of news, an item of information, a lump of machinery, a grain of rice, a slice of bread, a drop of blood, a block of wood, a cup of water, a packet of flour,* etc.

2 There are many unit words with special or idiomatic uses:
 a loaf of bread, a cube of sugar, a speck of dust, a blade of grass, a spark of electricity, a shout of joy, a stroke of luck, etc.

3 Group nouns are used before countable nouns to refer to things gathered together in a group: *group, heap, pile, bunch, mass, series, number, crowd.* Examples: *a group of trees, a pile*

221

of newspapers, a series of resolutions, a number of decisions. A number of really just means many. *Heap* and *pile* can be used with some uncountable nouns: *a heap of rubbish, a pile of wood*.

A verb often 'agrees' with the plural countable noun preceding it, not with the singular group noun:

A series of resolutions was passed *or* were passed.
A number of people were standing in the vestibule.

Special words are used with certain groups of animals: *a flock of sheep, a herd of cattle, a pack of dogs, a pride of lions*.

4 *Irregular Verbs in common use*

1 *Dictionary Form*	2 *Past Simple*	3 *Past Participle*	*Remarks*
be	was, were	been	*present tense*: am, is, are
bear	bore	born, borne	
beat	beat	beat	
begin	began	begun	
bend	bent	bent	
bet	bet, betted	bet, betted	
bind	bound	bound	
bite	bit	bitten	
bleed	bled	bled	
blow	blew	blown	
break	broke	broken	
breed	bred	bred	
bring	brought	brought	
build	built	built	
burn	burnt, burned	burnt, burned	
burst	burst	burst	
buy	bought	bought	
cast	cast	cast	*likewise* broadcast

222

1 *Dictionary Form*	2 *Past Simple*	3 *Past Participle*	*Remarks*
catch	caught	caught	
choose	chose	chosen	
cling	clung	clung	
come	came	come	*likewise* become, overcome
cost	cost	cost	
creep	crept	crept	
cut	cut	cut	
deal	dealt	dealt	
dig	dug	dug	
do	did	done	*likewise* undo, overdo
draw	drew	drawn	*likewise* overdraw, withdraw
dream	dreamt, dreamed	dreamt, dreamed	
drink	drank	drunk	
drive	drove	driven	
dwell	dwelt, dwelled	dwelt, dwelled	
eat	ate	eaten	
fall	fell	fallen	
feed	fed	fed	
feel	felt	felt	
fight	fought	fought	
find	found	found	
flee	fled	fled	
fling	flung	flung	
fly	flew	flown	
forbid	forbade	forbidden	
forget	forgot	forgotten	
get	got	got	
give	gave	given	
go	went	gone	*likewise* undergo

1 Dictionary Form	2 Past Simple	3 Past Participle	Remarks
grind	ground	ground	
grow	grew	grown	
hang	hung	hung	
have	had	had	
hear	heard	heard	
hide	hid	hidden	
hit	hit	hit	
hold	held	held	
hurt	hurt	hurt	
keep	kept	kept	
kneel	knelt	knelt	
know	knew	known	
lay	laid	laid	
lead	led	led	
lean	leant, leaned	leant, leaned	
leap	leapt	leapt	
learn	learnt, learned	learnt, learned	
leave	left	left	
lend	lent	lent	
let	let	let	
lie	lay	lain	lie *here means 'repose'*
light	lit, lighted	lit, lighted	
lose	lost	lost	
make	made	made	
mean	meant	meant	
meet	met	met	
pay	paid	paid	
put	put	put	
read	read	read	*pronounce the past simple and past participle in the same way as* 'red'

1 *Dictionary Form*	2 *Past Simple*	3 *Past Participle*	*Remarks*
ride	rode	ridden	
ring	rang	rung	
rise	rose	risen	
run	ran	run	
say	said	said	
see	saw	seen	
seek	sought	sought	
sell	sold	sold	
send	sent	sent	
set	set	set	
shake	shook	shaken	
shed	shed	shed	
shine	shone	shone	
shoot	shot	shot	
show	showed	shown, showed	
shrink	shrank	shrunk	
shut	shut	shut	
sing	sang	sung	
sink	sank	sunk	
sit	sat	sat	
sleep	slept	slept	
slide	slid	slid	
sling	slung	slung	
slink	slunk	slunk	
slit	slit	slit	
smell	smelt, smelled	smelt, smelled	
sow	sowed	sowed, sown	
speak	spoke	spoken	
speed	sped	sped	
spell	spelt, spelled	spelt, spelled	
spend	spent	spent	
spill	spilt, spilled	spilt, spilled	
spin	span	spun	

1 Dictionary Form	2 Past Simple	3 Past Participle	Remarks
spit	spat	spat	
split	split	split	
spoil	spoilt, spoiled	spoilt, spoiled	
spread	spread	spread	
spring	sprang	sprung	
stand	stood	stood	*likewise* understand, withstand
steal	stole	stolen	
stick	stuck	stuck	
sting	stung	stung	
strike	struck	struck	
string	strung	strung	
strive	strove	striven	
swear	swore	sworn	
sweep	swept	swept	
swell	swelled	swollen	
swim	swam	swum	
swing	swung	swung	
take	took	taken	*likewise* overtake, undertake
teach	taught	taught	
tear	tore	torn	
tell	told	.told	
think	thought	thought	
throw	threw	thrown	*likewise* overthrow
thrust	thrust	thrust	
tread	trod	trodden	
wake	woke	woken	*likewise* awake
wear	wore	worn	
weave	wove	woven	
weep	wept	wept	
win	won	won	
wind	wound	wound	*likewise* unwind

1 Dictionary Form	2 Past Simple	3 Past Participle	Remarks
wring	wrung	wrung	
write	wrote	written	*likewise* underwrite

Do and *go* have the third person singular present tense forms *does* and *goes* respectively.

5 Verb-Nouns in common use

1 The majority of *-ing* verb-nouns function both as verbs and nouns, but as nouns they are singular and uncountable only:

seeing, making, trying, giving, asking, receiving, hoping, using, eating, drinking, buying, selling, loving, dying, growing, falling, playing, parking, driving, singing, washing, etc.

2 Some *-ing* words not only function both as verbs and nouns, but as nouns they can be both uncountable and countable and can therefore have a plural in *-s*. Some have a special meaning in addition to the basic meaning, as indicated in brackets:

being, meaning, meeting, building (four walls and a roof), *feeling, suffering, failing* (weakness of character), *urging, pleading, teaching, blessing, sitting* (session of a committee, court, etc.), *hearing* (also 'session of a committee'), *cutting* (article cut from a newspaper), *holding* (block of shares in a company), *saving* (usually plural, meaning 'money saved'), *earning* (usually plural, meaning 'wages'), *carving* (a carved object), *posting, belonging* (the plural means 'possessions'), *greeting, shaving* (usually plural, meaning 'wood shaved off'), *doing, marking* (the plural means 'stains', or other kinds of disfigurement; the singular when it means 'correcting' has no plural), etc.

6 Prepositional Phrases

The most common prepositions are *in*, *at*, *on*, and *of*. They, and some others, are frequently used to form idiomatic phrases which function as adverbials of time, place, manner, etc., and as complements of *be*:

in (a) *Time Phrases. In* here refers to a point of time, though not a precise point of time, occurring within a longer period:

in 1960, in January, in the past, in the pre-colonial period, in the morning, in the evening, in the night, in the early days, in the middle of the week, in future.

(b) *Place Phrases.* Here the meaning of *in* is 'located within surrounding limits':

in the house, in his room, in a corner, in bed, in a taxi, in the bush, in the desert, in the ocean, in the sky, in Lagos (and other large cities), *in Zambia* (and other countries), *in the Middle East* (and other regions), *in the world.*

(c) *Other Phrases:*

in confusion, in debt, in difficulty; in exile, in pieces, in ruins, in trouble, in (a)good condition, in a crisis, in good health, in a good mood; in vain, in anger, in disgust, in surprise; in tears; in love; in conflict with . . ., in conversation with . . ., in honour of . . ., in memory of . . ., in reply to . . ., in search of . . ., in accordance with . . ., in addition, in that case, in those circumstances, in fact, in general, in my opinion; in order, in particular, in every respect, in that way, in a hurry; in a whisper, in a loud voice, in large letters, in a few words, in English; in black (meaning 'dressed in black clothes'), *in shorts, in African dress; in public, in private, in secret, in confidence; in a book, in a film, in a speech; in the rain* (e.g. *he likes walking in the rain*), *in the sun; in the head* (e.g. *he was wounded in the head*), *in the foot, in the stomach; in the Army, in the Public Service, in politics, in society,* and many others.

at (a) *Time Phrases. At* is used to refer to a precise point of clock time, and to other times that cannot be precisely specified:

at one o'clock, at 6.30; at dawn, at noon, at night; at breakfast, at lunchtime; at the weekend, at the beginning of the week; at times, at a sad time, at a difficult moment; at Christmas, at your Graduation.

(b) *Place Phrases. At* expresses the idea of location generally, or precise location:

at home, at school, at work; at his friend's (meaning 'at his friend's house'); *at table; at the bottom, at the top* (meaning *in the top part*); *at a meeting, at a conference, at a dance; at a distance, at a great height, at the end* (of a journey, for example); *at Government College* (and other buildings).

(c) *Other phrases*:

at first, at last, at least, at most, at once; at hand; at all costs, at any price, at a great risk, at my expense; at my suggestion; at war, at peace, at odds, at loggerheads; at any rate, at all (in *not at all*).

on (a) *Time Phrases*:

on Tuesday, on January 15th (and other days); *on his arrival, on a happy occasion, on your birthday, on time* (meaning 'punctually').

(b) *Other phrases*:

on no account, on purpose (meaning 'deliberately'), *on the whole* (meaning 'for the most part'), *on the spot*, (meaning 'in that very place'), *on foot, on his knees, on all fours, on his feet* (meaning 'walking about after an illness'), *on the radio, on television, on fire, on tenterhooks* (meaning 'anxious'); *on the condition that . . ., on the understanding that . . ., on your advice, on my authority; on board* (meaning 'inside a plane or boat').

by *by sea, by air; by car, by taxi, by train,* etc.; *by hand, by letter; by chance, by mistake, by all means, by the way.*

under	*under an obligation, under repair, under the agreement, under licence, under investigation, under examination* (but not an academic examination), *under the impression that . . ., under the guise of . . ., under way* ('starting').
with	*with difficulty, with pleasure, with reference to . . ., with the intention of . . ., with the exception of . . .*
out of	*out of work* ('jobless'), *out of order* ('not functioning'), *out of breath* ('breathless'), *out of turn, out of practice, out of control, out of date* ('old-fashioned'), *out of the question* ('not possible'), *out of pocket* ('without money').

7 Variable Class: Nouns and Verbs

Words which can function as nouns or verbs are extremely common. Here is a selection:

act, address, age, aid, aim, air, amount, answer, appeal, approach, arrest, attack, attempt, balance, bank, base, bath, beat, benefit, bite, blame, block, bolt, book, border, branch, break, bribe, burden, burn, burst, call, care, cash, cast, catch, cause, chain, challenge, change, charge, chat, check, circle, class, club, colour, comfort, command, comment, concern, conflict, consent, contact, contest, contract, cook, copy, corner, cost, cover, credit, cross, cry, cure, cut, damage, dance, date, deal, debate, decrease, defeat, delay, dish, dislike, display, dispute, document, draft, dream, dress, drink, drive, dust, edge, effect, end, escape, exchange, excuse, exercise, experience, face, fall, favour, fight, figure, file, find, fire, fish, fit, fix, flow, force, form, fuel, fund, gain, grade, grant, ground, guard, guide, handle, harm, harvest, head, heat, help, hold, hope, hunt, increase, influence, interest, interview, issue, judge, knock, land, lead, leave, lie, line, link, load, loan, lock, look, love, mail, march, mark, master, matter, measure, merit, mind, mistake, move, name, need, neglect, object, offer, oil, pack, pain, paint, part, pass, pay, place, plan, plant, point, pose, post, praise, present, print, profit, progress, project, protest, quarrel, question, raid, rain, rank, rate, reach, reason, record, reform, regard, register, remark, remedy, rent, repair, reserve, respect, rest, result, return, review, reward, risk, root, rule, rumour, sacrifice, say, scale, scheme, score, scratch, screen, search, seat, sentence, service, set, shape, share, show, side, sign, sink, sleep, smell, smile, smoke, sort, sound, spring, stage, stamp, stand, start, stick, stop, store, stress, study, subject, support, survey, suspect, switch, talk, taste, tax, telephone, test, touch, tour, trade, transfer, transport, trouble, trust, turn, type, value, visit, voice, vote, walk, wash, watch, water, wish, wonder, work.

8 The Sounds of English

The phonetic symbols used to represent the sounds of English (Received Pronunciation) are as follows. Examples are given of each sound as it appears in words.

Vowels:

/i:/	'ee' in *greet*, 'ea' in *treat*
/ɪ/	'i' in *simple*
/e/	'e' in *bet*
/æ/	'a' in *mat*
/u:/	'oo' in *moon*
/ʊ/	'oo' in *look*, 'u' in *bush*
/ɔ:/	'a' in *fall*, 'or' in *lord*
/ɒ/	'o' in *hot*, 'a' in *what*
/ɑ:/	'a' in *father*
/ʌ/	'u' in *stuff*, 'o' in *love*
/ɜ:/	'ir' in *first*, 'ur' in *burn*
/ə/	'e' in *happen*, 'o' in *reason*, 'a' in *plural*
/eɪ/	'a' in *late*, 'ai' in *pain*
/ɪə/	'ear' in *clear*
/eə/	'air' in *fair*, 'are' in *rare*
/aʊ/	'ou' in *mouth*, 'ow' in *now*
/ɔɪ/	'oi' in *oil*
/aɪ/	'i' in *time*, 'igh' in *night*
/əʊ/	'o' in *go*, 'ow' in *flow*
/ʊə/	'oor' in *poor*

Consonants:

/p/ 'p' in *pay*
/b/ 'b' in *beat*
/t/ 't' in *take*
/d/ 'd' in *do*
/k/ 'k' in *keep*, 'c' in *come*
/g/ 'g' in *get*
/tʃ/ 'ch' in *check*
/dʒ/ 'j' in *just*, 'dg' in *ledge*
/f/ 'f' in *first*
/v/ 'v' in *very*
/s/ 's' in *so*, 'ss' in *miss*
/z/ 'z' in *zero*, 's' in *has*
/ʃ/ 'sh' in *rush*
/ʒ/ 's' in *measure*
/θ/ 'th' in *think*, *both*
/ð/ 'th' in *the*, *that*
/n/ 'n' in *no*
/m/ 'm' in *my*
/ŋ/ 'ng' in *sing*
/l/ 'l' in *lip*
/r/ 'r' in *run*
/w/ 'w' in *we*
/j/ 'y' in *you*
/h/ 'h' in *help*

Exercises

These exercises are to some extent directly related to the errors identified and corrected in earlier chapters, but their primary objective is to provide practice in observing the general rules of English, which are broken when errors are committed. There will be little point in searching through the 650 items for the right answer in each case. Rather the student is advised to look when in doubt at the general rules stated at the beginning of each chapter or chapter sub-section, and at the relevant sections in Chapter 16.

The answers should be written on separate paper, not in the book itself.

Exercise 1 Nouns: irregular singulars and plurals

From the list of words at the top choose one word to fill the blank in each sentence, changing it where necessary to give the correct form. Each word must be used once.

bonus   thesis   rally   sheep   trousers   hero   thief   belief
people   radii   series   data   cargo   news   medium

1 Many _____ are expected at the naming ceremony.
2 _____ normally eat a lot of grass.
3 He took his _____ to the tailor to be mended.
4 Political parties are holding many _____ this year.
5 Your _____ all appear to be well-developed and well-written.
6 The drivers are applying for a _____.
7 We need to have more _____ before we can come to a conclusion.
8 The players were welcomed like _____.

9 Extend this _____ to point C beyond the circumference.
10 A long _____ of disputes followed.
11 The _____ of these ships have yet to be unloaded.
12 The _____ was reported to the police.
13 Newspapers are a very useful _____ of information.
14 The _____ took most of my things, but they left the television behind.
15 The _____ you hold are contrary to modern ideas.

Exercise 2 Nouns: singulars and plurals

Choose one of the two words in the brackets following each sentence to fill the blank in the sentence.

1 The bombs did much _____ to the city. (damage, damages)
2 The _____ of the two powers confronted each other. (army, armies)
3 The Party _____ resigned when they were found guilty of embezzlement. (Executive, Executives)
4 He showed his medal to many _____. (people, peoples)
5 The king died without _____, and was succeeded by his brother. (issue, issues)
6 For lack of _____ they could not pay us. (fund, funds)
7 A great task lies before the _____ of our country. (élite, élites)
8 He apologized for his _____ in writing to me. (delay, delays)
9 The land is marked by deep _____; crossing it is not easy. (depression, depressions)
10 They are too fat, and should try to lose _____ (weight, weights)
11 English and French are both based on the Roman _____. (alphabet, alphabets)
12 He saw the _____ approaching over the hill with their heavy artillery. (enemy, enemies)
13 Poor _____ caused him to make a bad investment. (advice, advices)

14 They were subjected to many _____ (restriction, restrictions)
15 He hopes to improve his physique by exercising with _____. (weight, weights)
16 Different _____ take up much of my time. (sport, sports)
17 I've heard a lot of _____ about it. (gossip, gossips)
18 He owns a mining company, but his brother is more interested in _____. (property, properties)
19 I wish I could help them; they are in deep _____. (depression, depressions)
20 She sued me for _____. (damage, damages)

Exercise 3 Nouns: countable and uncountable

Choose one of the words in the brackets following each sentence to fill the blank in the sentence.

1 He gave me an _____ but I have forgotten it. (information, instruction)
2 He went to buy a new _____ (underwear, shirt).
3 She spoke a _____ I could not understand. (slang, dialect)
4 A beautiful _____ met his eyes. (scene, scenery)
5 I issued him with a _____. (permit, permission)
6 He had to go to the hospital for _____ (an examination, a treatment)
7 He maintains that smoking is an evil _____. (practice, behaviour)
8 He was carrying a heavy _____. (luggage, load)
9 She washed her _____ under the tap. (hairs, hands)
10 He asked her to give him a _____. (loan, help)
11 He played a _____ on me, (fun, joke)
12 We have had a bad _____ this year. (weather, harvest)
13 I asked them to come and have a _____ with me. (meal, lunch)
14 I received a _____ today. (letter, mail)
15 She gave me a _____ for my attitude. (blame, rebuke)

16 The mechanic did a good _____ on my bicycle. (job, work)
17 I read a fine _____ last week. (novel, literature)
18 My country has a very stable _____. (currency, money)
19 The report was nothing but a _____. (rumour, hearsay)
20 He did me a great _____ by his visit. (honour, respect)

Exercise 4 Nouns: countable and uncountable

Use the word in brackets at the end of each sentence to fill the blank in the sentence, changing the form of the word where necessary.

1 A long series of _____ troubled Yorubaland in the 19th century. (war)
2 Lactose, dextrose, and fructose are all _____. (sugar)
3 There was a lot of _____ in their glasses. (foam)
4 Men who grow _____ are thought to be in mourning. (beard)
5 The Government has no more _____ to offer students. (scholarship)
6 He was practising different _____ of handwriting. (style)
7 They had no _____ left for the white line in the middle. (paint)
8 It was because of their bad _____ that they were suspended. (behaviour)
9 We spend much of our lives striving for power and _____. (position)
10 He feels that _____ manufacture will be a good business. (soap)

Exercise 5 Verb-nouns: singular and plural

Use the verb in brackets at the end of each sentence to form a noun ending in -ing or -ings which will fill the blank in the sentence.

1 He removed his _____ from the room. (belong)
2 They carried their _____ down to the stream. (wash)
3 We are not perfect; we all have our _____. (fail)

4 We heard a lot of _____ last night. (shoot)
5 I have little money left in my _____ account. (save)
6 We know he tells all those lies, but he never does so in our _____. (hear)
7 He suffered from a sense of injured _____. (feel)
8 The general _____ of the compound must be tidied. (surround)
9 He has just put up a lot of newspaper _____ on the board. (cut)
10 He always sends me a _____ card. (greet)

Exercise 6 Nouns and verbs, singular and plural

Study the following examples. The first sentence in each pair is rewritten in the plural:

Example 1: He ate his lunch. They ate their lunch.
Example 2: He brought a dog with him. They brought some dogs with them.

Now rewrite each of the following sentences, changing what can be changed to the plural:

1 He has installed new equipment.
2 The soldier put on his armour.
3 She likes to wear jewellery.
4 He has repaired all the machinery.
5 He sticks to his belief.
6 He put some sugar in his cup.
7 He entered into correspondence with the lecturer.
8 She had her dress mended.
9 He provided the information required of him.
10 She likes comfortable furniture.
11 The house lacks good plumbing.
12 The company wants to employ more staff.
13 He was accused of manslaughter.
14 He dropped his opposition to the plan.
15 She often listens to music.
16 His position had been carefully chosen.
17 He acted out of revenge.

18 He did harm to himself.
19 Our son is looking for work.
20 Your friend is soon going to obtain his degree.

Exercise 7 *Nouns and verbs, singular and plural*

Study the following example. The first sentence is rewritten in singular form:

Example: We collected our bags from the airport.
I collected my bag from the airport.

Now rewrite each of the following sentences, changing what can be changed to the singular:

1 They were ironing their trousers.
2 He did not know our whereabouts.
3 They cannot see properly when they remove their spectacles.
4 They stamped our passports.
5 These animals have long tails.
6 World powers have large fleets.
7 They live in the best quarters in the camp.
8 The roofs were covered with asbestos.
9 We were asked to buy fresh equipment.
10 These species of spider are found in North America.

Exercise 8 *Nouns and adjectives*

From the list of words at the top choose one word to fill the blank in each sentence, changing it where necessary to give the correct form. Each word must be used at least once; it is possible to use a word more than once.

innocent British rich particular junior infant alcoholic deaf poor good elderly German blind nomad subject unemployed dead criminal unsuitable

1 _____ should be brought to justice.
2 The _____ will soon be provided with work.
3 He invented a special hearing device to help the _____.

4 Braille is a system of writing used to help the _____.
5 Those men with cows are _____.
6 The _____ are a European people.
7 He had no passport but said he was a _____.
8 They were accused of the theft, but insisted they were _____.
9 He proposed Mafeke and Mbua, but I said they were _____.
10 He had no money himself, and people said that he was simply jealous of the _____.
11 The police told him to produce his _____.
12 It is for your own _____ that you are being disciplined.
13 He sold all his property and gave away the proceeds to the _____.
14 We are all _____ to the moral law.
15 They are all _____ to me; they cannot tell me what to do.
16 One should not speak ill of the _____.
17 The _____ in our midst are hereby warned that in future soft drinks only will be served.
18 They broke into his store and carried away thousands of cedis' worth of _____.
19 My children are all _____ prodigies; they will achieve great things in life.
20 No doubt the _____ spend much time recalling the days of their youth.

Exercise 9 Nouns used adjectivally

Study these examples:

Example 1 I saw *the hand* of *the man*. I saw the man's hand.
Example 2 I saw *the walls* of *the city*. I saw the city walls.
Example 3 I saw *a crowd* of *people*. NO CHANGE

Now do the following, putting one italicized noun phrase before the other in any suitable way, as suggested in Examples 1 and 2. If no such rearrangement can be made, give 'no change' as your answer.

1 I spoke to *the secretary* of *the Manager*.
2 She saw *the Governor* of *the State*.
3 We had *an evening* of *entertainment*.
4 I went to *the funeral* of *my friend*.
5 I wrote down *the number* of *the account*.
6 I passed through *the gates* of *the College*.
7 I reached *the top* of *the mountain*.
8 She was *a writer* of *thrillers*.
9 The treasure lay on *the bed* of *the ocean*.
10 I entered *the precincts* of *the factory*.
11 I visited *the headquarters* of *the Army*.
12 He went for *a walk* of *five miles*.
13 *The job* of *a traffic policeman* looks very tedious.
14 Man belongs to *the kingdom* of *animals*.
15 The sum of *the angles* of *a triangle* is 180°.
16 She sat down in *the library* of *the University*.
17 Many African *works* of *art* are kept in European museums.
18 We are looking for *a vehicle fifty years old*.
19 I spoke to *the Emir* of *Sanhaja*.
20 *Construction* of *buildings* can be a profitable business.

Exercise 10 Indefinite article

Rewrite the following sentences, using A or AN to fill the blank where necessary.

1 I expect to encounter _____ considerable trouble.
2 He went to have _____ bath.
3 They carried out _____ investigation into the crime.
4 He gave me _____ cause to believe he was right.
5 I went for _____ treatment of my injury.
6 I accused her of _____ extravagance.
7 I didn't have _____ chance to say hello to you.
8 He has turned to _____ crime now that he has left home.
9 He had _____ accident on his way to the match.
10 The case was dropped for lack of _____ evidence.
11 When you live in _____ community, you should obey its rules.

12 It gave me _____ surprise to know you were back.
13 He was in _____ despair when he heard of their defeat.
14 She was in _____ state of shock.
15 We will have to make _____ exchange of gifts.
16 It was a remark of _____ great significance.
17 He rose to make _____ speech of welcome.
18 The faculty of speaking is known as _____ speech.
19 The town is without _____ electricity and lies in darkness.
20 The Ottoman Empire was once _____ power of the first rank.

Exercise 11 *Definite article*

Rewrite the following sentences, using THE to fill the blank where necessary.

1 _____ slavery he found practised there appalled him.
2 He loved _____ company he had with him.
3 She practises _____ sculpture.
4 He was _____ shorter of the two.
5 An optimist believes in _____ progress.
6 We have had to change our ideas about _____ Early Man.
7 A nonconformist is one who sets himself against _____ society.
8 _____ songs I heard last night were delightful.
9 The size of the city does not give _____ room for any further development.
10 _____ human management is difficult.
11 _____ slavery was practised on a large scale in those days.
12 He loves _____ excitement of all kinds.
13 He is going to study _____ engineering for his degree.
14 _____ space travel will become more frequent in future.
15 He travelled in _____ company with his friends.
16 His illness was diagnosed as _____ bilharzia.

17 _____ X-rays are dangerous to living tissue.
18 _____ drought we have had this year is very serious.
19 I came to _____ conclusion that you had forgotten me.
20 _____ soil erosion threatens agriculture in many parts of Africa.

Exercise 12 Definite article

Rewrite the following sentences, using THE to fill the blank where necessary.

1 He flew over _____ Pacific Ocean.
2 They built a bridge over _____ River Zambezi.
3 At last we reached _____ Lake Tanganyika.
4 Jos is the capital of _____ Plateau State.
5 Singapore is very close to _____ Equator.
6 The nearest planet to the Sun is _____ Mercury.
7 Jamaica lies on the north side of _____ Caribbean Sea.
8 Nairobi is not far from _____ Mount Kenya.
9 _____ United Nations Organization was founded in 1945.
10 We went for a walk along _____ Macaulay Street.
11 He is a graduate of _____ University of Harvard.
12 My daughter has been admitted to _____ St. Monica's College.
13 He has travelled to _____ Far East on a recruitment exercise.
14 Where on the map do you find _____ Greenland?
15 He is in charge of _____ Equatorial Province.
16 _____ Trans-Africa Highway has become a reality.
17 _____ Pope will visit our country next year.
18 _____ Atlas Mountains lie in North Africa.
19 They live in _____ Kalahari Desert.
20 Their electoral prospects have been improved through their merger with _____ PPP.

Exercise 13 Indefinite and definite articles

Rewrite the following sentences, using A or AN or THE to fill the blank where necessary. In some cases nothing may be needed to fill the blank, in which case the blank should be omitted.

1 He wants to study for _____ Ph.D.
2 I offered _____ large reward to anyone who could find her.
3 He always gets up at _____ dawn.
4 He has a great interest in _____ social science.
5 Our farmers practise _____ crop rotation.
6 I have _____ objection to raise.
7 Because they offered _____ resistance, they were killed.
8 _____ mythology of the Ancient Egyptians is very interesting.
9 I am gratified by _____ admiration you have expressed.
10 He says he will take up _____ carpentry to pass the time.

Exercise 14 Determiners and pronouns

Choose one of the suggested alternatives to fill the blank in each sentence.

1 Fifty men went out to sea. Five came back. Thus _____ came back.
   (a) some (b) several (c) most (d) only a few
2 They overran all the country except the capital and its neighbourhood. Thus they overran _____ of the country.
   (a) all (b) most (c) part (d) several
3 Twenty birds were in the cage, but six of them were dead by the morning. Thus _____ of them had died.
   (a) several (b) a few (c) most (d) more
4 He asked for cigarettes, but I said there were _____.
   (a) some (b) none (c) a few (d) several
5 Since there are _____ people present, we can start the meeting.
   (a) few (b) a few (c) little (d) much
6 The meat weighed two kilos, and I asked him to add an extra kilo. So I asked him to give me _____ meat.
   (a) another (b) other (c) more (d) many

7 My father was at the farm, and my mother had gone to the market; so _____ of them was available.
(a) neither (b) both (c) either (d) none

8 There's _____ ventilation in this room; that's why you don't breathe well.
(a) few (b) a little (c) little (d) much

9 Of the ten-storey building, five storeys were gutted by the fire. So _____ of the building was destroyed.
(a) much (b) most (c) a little (d) several

10 He gave me a job and he gave my friend a job. So he gave a job to _____ of us.
(a) everyone (b) all (c) two (d) each

Exercise 15 Determiners and pronouns

A Choose words from this list to fill the blanks in the sentences that follow. Each word must be used and each must be used only once.

those other a ours either whole five my many all

1 He has spent _____ _____ money.
2 _____ _____ city was affected.
3 I could not see _____ of _____ tickets.
4 _____ of the letters are _____
5 _____ _____ people besides Juba were injured.

B (Instructions as previous exercise.)

our any every most two a some none few three

1 _____ people were hurrying; a _____ were just strolling.
2 It rains heavily _____ or _____ days.
3 Whenever she hears _____ dog barking, she feels afraid.
4 I couldn't see _____ Ugandans, but you said there were _____.
5 _____ of _____ expected guests may arrive.

C (Instructions as previous exercises.)

much a any several whole another this the all
more

1 _____ _____ houses will be connected.
2 They said he had drunk _____ _____ crate of beer.
3 _____ of _____ land is now useless.
4 I asked him _____ questions, but he didn't reply to
_____.
5 You can supply _____ milk _____ time.

D (Instructions as previous exercises.)

more their half much neither that some those
many next

1 _____ of _____ fuel has been consumed.
2 They decided to give _____ _____ son African
names.
3 _____ of _____ typewriters is functioning.
4 _____ has been said about _____ things.
5 _____ _____ sand must be added to make the
cement good.

Exercise 16 Pronouns and possessives

Choose one of the suggested alternatives to fill the blank in each
sentences.

1 The Club calls on all _____ members to contribute.
  (a) her (b) his (c) its (d) their
2 Mary asked me to give it to her mother, but I gave it to
  _____ father instead.
  (a) her (b) his (c) its
3 My country calls me; I am ready to die for _____.
  (a) him (b) her (c) them
4 The African extended family gives security to _____
  members.
  (a) his (b) her (c) its (d) their
5 Joseph and Judith trust _____.
  (a) themselves (b) each other (c) anyone (d) everyone

6 I approve of _____ you have done.
   (a) all what (b) everything (c) anyone (d) everyone
7 They should criticise _____ before criticising others.
   (a) one another (b) each other (c) themselves
8 This wood is infested with termites; I will soon replace
   _____.
   (a) them (b) it (c) him
9 He was no friend of _____.
   (a) me (b) mine (c) we (d) us
10 _____ remained only two pieces of meat.
   (a) It (b) They (c) She (d) There

Exercise 17 Relative pronouns

Study these examples:

Example 1 I have come with someone. He will interpret for
you.
I have come with someone who will interpret for
you.

Example 2 Here is a knife. You can use it.
Here is a knife which you can use.

Now join the two sentences in each of the following pairs with
the aid of any suitable relative pronoun:

1 I have a friend called Johnson. He walks five miles every
day.
2 The things belonged to a shepherd. His whereabouts were
unknown.
3 She left him for her boy-friend. That did not surprise us.
4 I have come with a spanner. You can use it to tighten the
bolts.
5 There were riots also in Kassani. So far we have received
few details of them.
6 All the things are going to be carried away and either sold
or burned. You left them in your room.
7 The landlady stood on the stairs and shouted. The instructions of the landlady had been ignored.
8 We must now go and call on Mr Matatu. Your brother's
life was saved thanks to him.

9 I have found the bunch of keys. You said you were looking for them.
10 He stood under the tree. A spirit dwelt in it according to local belief.

Exercise 18 Continuous forms

Give the correct form of the verb in brackets.

1 He (make) a long speech, but no one is listening.
2 The bus (belong) to me, but I don't use it.
3 The baby (sleep), so don't make a noise.
4 The sun (shine), so there won't be any rain.
5 He (have) a hat, but he is not wearing it.
6 Aeroplanes sometimes (fly) very low, and many people look anxious.
7 This egg (seem) bad, so don't eat it.
8 The packet (contain) 50 tablets; take 3 per day.
9 When you (reach) my age, you will start fearing old age.
10 I (see) that you are better.

Exercise 19 Irregular verbs

Give the correct form of the verb in brackets.

1 He (fly) as far as Khartoum, then turned back.
2 She always (let) us read.
3 He (forbid) you to do that, but still you did it.
4 I (cut) my finger when I was opening that tin.
5 They (spend) a lot of money when they went to London.
6 It was his proposal which (split) the committee.
7 She (shed) tears when she learned of your misfortune.
8 He felt so cold that he (light) a fire.
9 We (meet) last Monday at the Post Office.
10 He (shut) his shop last night and travelled home.

Exercise 20 Irregular verbs

Give the correct form of the word or words in brackets.

1 I (creep) quietly down the corridor, not wanting to wake them.

2 He has taken his soundings and (choose) Adetola as his running-mate.

3 I (now, hide) your cassettes so that you won't be able to play them.

4 Here he is: he (just, drive) one thousand kilometres.

5 She (cast) her vote for me, but still I wasn't successful.

6 He (put) on a record and they began dancing.

7 His foot was very (swell) after the injury.

8 They (strike) back at the enemy and defeated them decisively.

9 He (kneel) down and gave thanks to God.

10 The sun (already, rise) before we awoke.

Exericse 21 Use of auxiliaries: questions and negatives

From the list of words at the top choose one word to fill the blank in each sentence. Each word must be used at least once. Some words may be used more than once.

is are was were do does did has have had
isn't aren't wasn't weren't don't doesn't didn't hasn't

1 There goes Mr Murumba. _____ you know him?

2 She is miserable because her friend _____ speaking to her any more.

3 What car _____ he bought? Let's see it.

4 Why _____ the steward greet you when you passed him? Is he annoyed?

5 I know he runs a taxi, but what gain _____ he make?

6 I am offering her a lot of money for the car, but she says she _____ want to sell it.

7 I could hear a lot of noise coming from your room; _____ you arguing with each other?

8 They _____ supposed to put up a building here; that is why it was pulled down again.

9 He said he wrote to me but I am quite sure he _____.

10 _____ you surprised when he put the book in front of you?

11 _____ the trees blossom at this time of the year?

12 _____ they going to visit him, or will he visit them first?

13 How many Christmas cards _____ you sent?
14 What _____ it that made him frown like that?
15 It was unusual for you to miss that meeting: _____ you
   not received the invitation?
16 I _____ suppose you have ever had a bonus.
17 What _____ the clock say when you left the house?
18 _____ the lecture going to be held, or has it been
   cancelled?
19 If you _____ ready, get somebody else to go.
20 He argues that our people eat pork, but of course we
   _____.
21 _____ it ever occurred to you that you may have
   offended her?
22 It _____ appropriate for you to speak the way you did.
23 _____ it been unusually hot today?
24 _____ you buy the newspaper, as I requested?
25 When _____ you take your next test?

Exercise 22 Tag questions

Fill the blank in each of the following sentences with the
appropriate tag question.

Example 1 He is at home, _____? Answer: ISN'T HE.
Example 2 She didn't fall, _____? Answer: DID SHE.

 1 He plays football, _____?
 2 They can't swim, _____?
 3 We don't have any meat left, _____?
 4 They will stay for a whole week, _____?
 5 She wouldn't believe you, _____?
 6 I scored seventeen, _____?
 7 He cut his finger, _____?
 8 It isn't five o'clock yet, _____?
 9 They are still being used, _____?
10 The office was closed today, _____?
11 We were warmly received, _____?
12 You won't leave immediately, _____?
13 You'll still be there, _____?

14 He has gone, _____?
15 The weather's still bad, _____?
16 It seems to be slowing down, _____?
17 You've not got any message yet, _____?
18 He'd spend everything, _____?
19 He doesn't know the way, _____?
20 They're bound to ask you, _____?

Exercise 23 Various tenses

Choose one of the suggested alternatives to fill the blank in each of the following sentences.

1 He _____ to Nigeria ten years ago.
   (a) has come (b) came (c) is come (d) is coming
2 He _____ in Kenya since 1960 and is still there.
   (a) had lived (b) lives (c) is living (d) has lived
3 She _____ her name down and took a card.
   (a) writes (b) has written (c) was writing (d) wrote
4 So you _____ the Police Force; I hope you will like it.
   (a) join (b) have joined (c) are joined (d) were joining.
5 She _____ an interview and cannot see you at present.
   (a) conducts (b) conducted (c) is conducting (d) had conducted
6 It _____ me a shock when I heard of his accident.
   (a) gave (b) has given (c) gives (d) was giving
7 They _____ as soon as they heard of their father's death.
   (a) were returning (b) returned (c) return
   (d) are returning
8 It was a peaceful afternoon and everyone _____.
   (a) had slept (b) has slept (c) slept (d) was sleeping
9 They _____ many hardships before they were released in 1920.
   (a) suffer (b) suffered (c) have suffered
   (d) are suffering
10 Whenever he put the light on, someone _____ to disturb him.
   (a) came (b) comes (c) has come (d) had come

11 Liver _____ less than ordinary meat and is highly nutritious.
   (a) has cost (b) costs (c) had cost (d) cost
12 He _____ to Dar-es-Salaam tomorrow, so he will have to get to bed early.
   (a) is travelling (b) was travelling (c) has travelled
   (d) would travel
13 These deposits _____ millions of years ago.
   (a) laid (b) lay (c) are being laid (d) were laid
14 He _____ my shoes but did not use polish.
   (a) cleans (b) is cleaning (c) has cleaned (d) will clean
15 Clouds _____; it will soon rain.
   (a) gathered (b) gather (c) were gathering (d) are gathering
16 That fire _____ my house if you are not careful.
   (a) destroys (b) will destroy (c) destroyed (d) is destroying
17 The Sun _____ surrounded by nine major planets.
   (a) was (b) is being (c) has been (d) was been (e) is
18 He must _____ if his car is there.
   (a) arrive (b) be arriving (c) have arrived (d) arrived
19 A flourescent bulb _____ more light and is more economical.
   (a) gives (b) gave (c) had given (d) was giving
20 There is a war scare and people in border villages _____ evacuated.
   (a) were (b) are (c) have been (d) were being (e) had been

Exercise 24 Perfect tenses

Give the correct form of the word or words in brackets.

1 I (already, go) to sleep when he knocked at the door.
2 He said that he (often, see) them digging holes.
3 I believe you (now, receive) the letter I posted last month.
4 It (explain) to me several times, but still I can't understand it.

5 The bridge (collapse) before the team could arrive.
6 She (have) nightmares all this week; I trust she is now less disturbed.
7 Long before aeroplanes were invented, man (make) several attempts to fly.
8 He may (ask) me, but I have forgotten.
9 I hear that you (receive) some bad news on Monday.
10 We were not happy because our team (defeat).
11 An announcement (make, just) over the radio, saying that all flights are suspended.
12 If he (really, say) such things, he would have been punished.
13 He (read) for five hours; he must be tired.
14 What (happen) to him? He looks so neat and tidy these days.
15 Heavy rain (fall), and the roads were impassable.
16 There was excitement everywhere: the presidential party (just, arrive).
17 If you (ever, insult), you will appreciate how I feel.
18 He (feel) better in the last few days, so you may see him tomorrow.
19 It angered me to discover how little work (do), but I decided to overlook it.
20 Now that those visitors (go), I can sit down and rest for a while.

Exercise 25 Various tenses

Fill the blanks in the following passage with suitable words derived from the verb shown in brackets in each case:

The Federal Government _____ (release) 80,000 doses of vaccines for the prevention and treatment of rinderpest in Sokoto State. The State Commissioner for Agriculture _____ (tell) journalists in Sokoto on Monday that a total of 125,000 doses of the vaccine _____ (still, expect) from the Federal Government. All these _____ (not, be) enough, however, because according to him there _____ (be) up to four million cattle in the state. The Commissioner _____ (announce) that the Ministry _____ (succeed) in vaccinating

more than one million cattle since the outbreak of the disease
_____ (first, report) last November. He _____ (add) that
the Government _____ (now, prepare) for a statewide
inoculation of cattle from the first week of next month.

Exercise 26 Active and passive

Convert the following active sentences to passive sentences,
using the words italicized in the active sentence as the subject
of the passive sentence.

Example: Someone opened *the door*.
          The door was opened by someone. *or*
          The door was opened.

1 Wind blows *the seeds* about.
2 Our cameramen filmed *the scene*.
3 They have closed *this road* to traffic.
4 It surprised *him* that the locusts had returned.
5 They will abolish *all restrictions*.
6 People often see *you* walking in the rain.
7 They are going to conduct *a fresh census*.
8 We are seeking *a solution* to this growing problem.
9 They were keeping *me* in a dark cell.
10 They are likely to charge *anyone they catch* with fraud.
11 He reported *the loss* to the authorities.
12 Helen rang *the bell*.
13 You must speak *your words* in a whisper.
14 They sank *one of our ships*.
15 They are shooting *three of the conspirators* at dawn tomorrow.
16 They were not teaching *science subjects* any more.
17 They weave *this cloth* on a traditional type of loom.
18 It pleases *us* to get letters from you.
19 He had thrust *some papers* into a pigeon-hole.
20 If Amaka wins *this round*, the victory will be ours.

Exercise 27 Active and passive

Use the word in brackets at the end of each sentence to fill the
blank in each sentence, changing its form where necessary:
 1 The transmitter _____ on high ground. (situate)
 2 The battery _____ of four cells. (comprise)

3 The box _____ of three compartments. (consist)
4 If the meeting _____ this morning, I shall be there. (hold)
5 He _____ to have escaped during the night. (believe)
6 If he _____ he must be given first-aid. (wound)
7 The words _____ to you, so study them closely. (refer)
8 They want the next conference to _____ in the capital. (hold)
9 The matter will _____ to you for your consideration. (refer)
10 If my watch _____ again, I shall take it for repair. (stop)

Exercise 28 Various auxiliaries

Choose one of the suggested alternatives to fill the blank in each sentence.

1 You _____ not be happy in your new situation, but you will have to bear it.
(a) may (b) shall (c) could (d) must (e) need
2 He _____ find it easy to pass Economics, since he has studied it for a long time.
(a) used to (b) shall (c) should (d) won't (e) ought
3 You _____ try to help yourself; no one else can help you.
(a) need (b) would (c) had to (d) must (e) shouldn't
4 That radio _____ be mine; mine has aerial.
(a) shall (b) mustn't (c) won't (d) can't (e) used to
5 He _____ recover his voice, but don't let him try to sing again.
(a) will (b) shall (c) would (d) shouldn't (e) can't
6 He _____ to be presented with this certificate, but his name is not on it.
(a) should (b) used (c) have (d) was (e) isn't
7 _____ you come and sit here? I want to practise my Swahili.
(a) Shouldn't (b) May (c) Won't (d) Don't
(e) Should

8 I know I _____ read more, but I am just too tired.
   (a) ought to (b) may (c) can't (d) would (e) can

9 If I were you I _____ ask your father to help you.
   (a) can (b) need to (c) would (d) am to (e) mustn't

10 I _____ not understand at the time he married her why
   he didn't marry the eldest daughter.
   (a) would (b) need (c) should (d) could (e) shall

11 It _____ be taken for repair after all; it's working again.
   (a) couldn't (b) mightn't (c) would (d) needn't

12 Supplies _____ be dropped by aircraft; the people would
   have perished otherwise.
   (a) had to (b) should (c) must (d) shall (e) can

13 Your President _____ invited; he will feel insulted at
   being left out.
   (a) must have been (b) should have been (c) would
   have been

14 It _____ to surprise me to see him every day; now I
   know he was visiting his grandmother.
   (a) use (b) ought (c) is (d) used (e) had

15 'The Director wishes to speak to you,' said the secretary to
   her boss. '_____ I ask him to come in?'
   (a) Would (b) Shall (c) Can (d) May (e) Will

16 _____ you go already? I'm quite sure you don't need to
   go for another hour.
   (a) Can (b) Must (c) Would (d) Shall (e) Wouldn't

17 He said he _____ allow you to go to the dance, provided
   you return early.
   (a) will (b) shall (c) shouldn't (d) won't (e) used to

18 I detest poetry, but I _____ like novels, and often read
   them.
   (a) might (b) must (c) do (d) would (e) can

19 It _____ be Mr Salim over there; it couldn't possibly be
   anyone else.
   (a) has to (b) would (c) shall (d) may (e) can't

20 I _____ come and speak, but I can't promise you.
   (a) daren't (b) needn't (c) shall (d) had to (e) might

Exercise 29 Will and would

Fill the blank in each of the following sentences with either *will* or *would*:

1 The car _____ collect you whenever you are ready.
2 He said as early as 1900 that independence _____ come.
3 If only it _____ stop raining, we could go out.
4 The Post Office has declared that as from tomorrow there _____ be no more sales of stamps.
5 I _____ go there, but please accompany me.
6 The plane _____ leave at 5 p.m. That is what she has just said.
7 I hope you _____ not feel disappointed if we don't invite you.
8 In future, everyone _____ take annual leave at the same time; this is the new policy.
9 I _____ not have asked you if I knew you couldn't come.
10 It _____ be better if you took your son away from this school.

Exercise 30 Time and condition clauses

Choose one of the suggested alternatives to fill the blank in each sentence.

1 When you _____ from him, let me know.
   (a) hear   (b) might have heard   (c) must have heard
2 After the plane _____ taken off, we shall serve lunch.
   (a) will have   (b) must have   (c) might have   (d) has
3 If he _____ to bite you, give him a good beating.
   (a) tried   (b) will try   (c) tries   (d) would try
4 As soon as the matter _____ to you, take it up with the authorities.
   (a) is reported   (b) reported   (c) must have been reported
   (d) would have been reported   (e) must be reported
5 Provided you _____ to the market very soon, we shall be able to eat early enough.
   (a) have gone   (b) would go   (c) should go   (d) go
6 Whenever he _____ with his new car, I shall be delighted.

(a) will arrive   (b) might have arrived   (c) might arrive
(d) arrives   (e) shall arrive
7 He _____ by now; I can hear all the people shouting.
   (a) would arrive   (b) must have arrived   (c) arrives
   (d) is to arrive   (e) must arrive
8 By the time the plane reaches Harare, it _____ in the air for twelve hours.
   (a) has been   (b) will have been   (c) will be   (d) is
   (e) was
9 As soon as he _____ home, he goes to bed and rests.
   (a) got   (b) gets   (c) must get   (d) will get   (e) would get
10 On the day you _____ your project, we shall celebrate.
   (a) must have finished   (b) might have finished   (c) would finish   (d) finish   (e) finished

Exercise 31 Prepositions

Choose one of the following prepositions: *in*, *at*, *on*, *by*, to fill the blank in each sentence.

1 She was lying _____ the middle of the road.
2 _____ evening most of the guests had left.
3 He felt lonely _____ the early part of his life.
4 He was still _____ exile when he heard of the coup.
5 Come and see me _____ one o'clock, which is when I return from lunch.
6 _____ January next year I shall have been working for the Government for ten years.
7 I listened to him _____ your request.
8 I will come and see you _____ the evening.
9 I looked for you _____ Monday morning in the town.
10 They are already eating; _____ one o'clock nothing will remain.

Exercise 32 Prepositions

Fill the blank in each of the following sentences with any suitable preposition.

1 _____ a long journey ahead of him, he set out early.

257

2 They all refused to co-operate _____ Kofi.
3 _____ lack of spare parts they declined to do the job.
4 She is suffering _____ a serious illness.
5 Drive slowly _____ the junction, then accelerate.
6 I like tennis, but I am seriously _____ practice.
7 We are _____ no obligation to remove it.
8 I could not see the game very well; a tall man was standing _____ me.
9 The tortoise made its way _____ difficulty through the grass.
10 He had a garden _____ the back of his house.

Exercise 33 Prepositions

Choose one of the following prepositions: *on*, *in*, *at*, *with*, to fill the blank in each sentence.

1 He was _____ bed when I arrived.
2 She went to the market _____ foot.
3 _____ further consideration I will release you.
4 He was standing _____ the edge of the stream.
5 He was standing _____ the bridge looking into the water.
6 Fire broke out _____ one of the dormitories.
7 I met them _____ the junction.
8 _____ his departure he gave me fifty shillings.
9 _____ this rate you will never finish the work.
10 No doubt you will recover _____ the end.
11 Do such things happen _____ the twentieth century?
12 Please move your table; it is _____ my way.
13 It was _____ difficulty that he raised the money.
14 He was _____ a bad mood and spoke sharply.
15 I am always in favour of _____-the-job training.
16 She grew up _____ Lesotho.
17 _____ all the assistance he received he still failed.
18 Whenever you see anyone _____ difficulty, do your best to help.
19 He lived _____ London for many years.

20 We are always _____ conflict with the Ministry of Transport.

Exercise 34 Common prepositional phrases

Choose a word from the list of words at the top to fill the blank in each of these sentences. Each word must be used at least once; some words may be used more than once.

whole way light attempt odds course time
times impression cause board level confidence
context opinion

1 On the _____ we had a good journey.
2 In the _____ of what you have told me I will think again.
3 By the _____, can you tell me what this means?
4 In the _____ to recover his balance, he slipped.
5 You will find yourselves at _____ with everybody if you persist.
6 At _____ I have little desire to eat.
7 He was injured in the _____ of duty.
8 By coming in _____ he got a good seat.
9 He was under the _____ that I had granted him permission.
10 No smoking is allowed on _____.
11 This matter will have to be handled at the administrative _____.
12 He speaks with great _____, and will be a politician one day.
13 He decided to take up the _____ of the oppressed and exploited peasants.
14 In my _____ none of the prisoners should be released.
15 He said he had encountered many obstacles on the _____.
16 These are words used in the _____ of scientific discussion.
17 We say many things in _____ which soon become public.
18 By the _____ you get home you will be exhausted.

259

19 He passed his driving-test at the first _____.
20 We hope to improve our facilities in due _____.

Exercise 35 Time adverbials

Choose one of the suggested alternatives to fill the blank in each sentence.

1 I haven't been there of _____: let's go there tomorrow.
   (a) late (b) recent (c) recently (d) lately
2 I came to live here _____, and don't yet know many people.
   (a) lately (b) of recent (c) later (d) recently
3 Your application form reached us too _____.
   (a) recent (b) lately (c) late (d) later
4 He has been here _____, and is getting very impatient.
   (a) since (b) long ago (c) before long (d) a long time
5 Please come back _____; we shall not start the registration for about an hour.
   (a) later (b) after (c) at length (d) presently
6 It was a long time _____ that I last played any football.
   (a) before (b) since (c) previous (d) ago (e) till now
7 She is in mourning for her _____ husband.
   (a) letter (b) late (c) later (d) recent
8 He was working on the job for five hours. _____ he had a good sleep.
   (a) After (b) Before (c) Afterwards (d) Previously
9 She arrived home on January 10th. _____ her sister also arrived.
   (a) The second day (b) On the second day (c) The next day (d) Next tomorrow (e) Tomorrow
10 He will be here _____, so you won't have to wait long.
   (a) shortly (b) immediately (c) soonest (d) at present
11 This is a very arid region where it _____ rains.
   (a) always (b) seldom (c) occasionally (d) sometimes

Exercise 36 Adjectives and adverbs

Choose a word from the list at the top to fill the blank in each of the sentences below, giving the word the correct form as required.

Example (using *clear*): He is _____ the best man for the job.
Answer: Clearly.

Each word must be used at least once; some words may be used more than once.

bad sharp stupid clear delicious likely exciting sour
eager hard careful fast angry

1 He _____ said that he would take orders from no one.
2 The meat smells _____; throw it away.
3 Warm this soup this morning, or it will turn _____.
4 He turned his car _____ to the right.
5 He looks rather _____: surely he will not perform well.
6 Your cake tastes _____.
7 You must try _____ to finish this in time.
8 The applicant looked at me _____ when I said there was a vacancy.
9 It doesn't seem _____ that he will go today.
10 Consider the matter _____ before taking a decision.
11 He _____ ever combs his hair.
12 Her voice came over the radio loud and _____.
13 I found last night's film most _____.
14 The little boy was so _____ injured that he was in hospital for weeks.
15 She writes so _____ that she is always the first to finish.

Exercise 37 Adverbs of degree

Choose a word or phrase from the list at the top to fill the blank in each of the sentences. Some words may be used more than once.

too so very enough somehow rather so much
very much

1 She spoke _____ quietly that no one could hear her.
2 You are _____ fond of exposing other people's secrets; it must stop.

3 It wasn't good _____ to be included in the exhibition.
4 I was _____ pleased to hear you had obtained your certificate.
5 She mended it _____, though she had no scissors.
6 The film was _____ amusing, and we stayed until the end.
7 You are speaking _____ fast; try to slow down a bit.
8 He looked _____ miserable that I thought he would burst into tears.
9 He ran _____ water that he had none left in the tank.
10 I _____ like the colour, though my wife says it's too bright.
11 The ice-cream is _____ cold for me to eat at present.
12 He _____ managed to find out that I was inside.
13 I have eaten _____ recently that I must go on a diet.
14 We didn't enjoy the dance _____; few people were there.
15 _____ than ask you to repeat it, I will give you another chance.

Exercise 38 Comparatives

Rewrite the following sentences, using the word MORE to fill the blank when possible. Leave out the blank when MORE cannot be used.

1 Your car performs _____ better than mine does.
2 His story is _____ credible, now that we know some of the facts.
3 The floods were much _____ severe than we imagined.
4 Increase the sound _____; I cannot hear the music.
5 My love for you becomes _____ intense as the years pass.
6 The flames rose _____ higher and higher.
7 She can run _____ faster than I can.
8 She teaches _____ effectively than most of her colleagues.
9 Both songs have sweet melodies, but this one has the _____ moving words.
10 That spray is very effective, but this one is _____ superior.

262

Exercise 39 Conjunctions

Choose one of the suggested alternatives to fill the blank in each of these sentences.

1 _____ he has secured a good job in your company, why is he applying elsewhere?
   (a) Hence   (b) For the fact that   (c) Since   (d) Though
2 _____ I know, nobody has seen any leopards in this area.
   (a) So far   (b) So far as   (c) If   (d) Provided
3 Do not offer him money _____ he asks you for it.
   (a) as if   (b) provided   (c) in order that   (d) unless
4 His eyesight is poor; _____ he finds office work difficult.
   (a) since   (b) hence   (c) although   (d) though
5 I will say nothing _____ you first reveal those names.
   (a) unless   (b) except   (c) as soon as   (d) because
6 _____ he had insufficient qualifications, he was denied admission.
   (a) Hence   (b) For the fact that   (c) Being that   (d)As
7 _____ him in the crowd, I would have told you at once.
   (a) Had it been I saw   (b) If I saw   (c) Had I seen
   (d) Should I see
8 He had no quarrel with anybody; _____ his sudden departure came as a great surprise.
   (a) although   (b) when   (c) hence   (d) as   (e) because
9 _____ I have bought all this land, I must build something.
   (a) Being that   (b) Hence   (c) Except   (d) Now that
10 _____ lazy he may be, he is not unintelligent.
   (a) Though   (b) If   (c) So   (d) However   (e) Since

Exercise 40 Phrasal verbs: up and back

Rewrite the following sentences, using UP or BACK to fill the blank when possible; otherwise leave out the blank.

1 There is not enough room in front of you; you will have to reverse _____.

2 She doesn't have the temperament to cope _____ with a crisis.
3 That's a good idea. Follow it _____, and we'll see what the boss says.
4 I asked him to pick me _____ at four o'clock.
5 He leaned _____ in the chair and put his feet on the table.
6 The King was restored _____ to his throne after a long period of exile.
7 He drew _____ plans for mass evacuation.
8 I am off to the site now; it will be lunchtime before I return _____.
9 She didn't know she had been recorded until I played the cassette _____.
10 He is always ready to pick _____ a quarrel with somebody.
11 Shakespeare wrote _____ nearly forty plays.
12 I told him to roll _____ the windows; rain was coming.
13 I drew _____ his attention to the discrepancy in the figures.
14 You should learn to give _____ what you borrow from people.
15 Let's not discuss that now; bring it _____ at the next meeting.

Exercise 41 Prepositions

Rewrite the following sentences, filling the blank in each with one of the following where necessary: *for, of, on, with*. In some cases none of the above is required, in which case the blank should be omitted.

1 They presented their demand _____ additional staff.
2 We advocate _____ a complete reorganization.
3 He submitted a report _____ the crime.
4 I asked for a fresh supply _____ ink.
5 They lack _____ many amenities in their school.
6 They had to operate _____ him without delay.
7 I asked them to supply us _____ more paper.

8 I reported _____ his dismissal to the Minister.
9 He expressed no regrets _____ his rudeness.
10 You must comply _____ all the regulations.
11 I advise you to inform _____ the Dean immediately.
12 He is a trader, and deals _____ general provisions.
13 He has not yet answered _____ the query.
14 Her request _____ more money was turned down.
15 You can't rely _____ him.
16 Calculate how much interest I will get _____ this amount.
17 In his work he deals _____ all kinds of people.
18 He has felt ashamed _____ himself since his expulsion.
19 He puts the interest _____ his fellow-citizens first.
20 They are demanding _____ a ban on imported goods.
21 He laid stress _____ the importance of self-discipline.
22 How do you account _____ the discrepancy in these figures?
23 He was charged _____ having tried to pervert the course of justice.
24 She was suspected _____ having poisoned her husband.
25 The Minister in his speech stressed _____ the danger of forgetting about agriculture.

Exercise 42 *Prepositional verbs and verb patterns*

Fill the blank in each of the following sentences with the aid of the words in brackets.

1 He insisted _____ the manuscript. (read)
2 I objected _____ another X-ray. (have)
3 I regretted _____ you there. (not, find)
4 She was about _____ a fire, but I stopped her. (light)
5 I should like _____ from you. (hear)
6 We were annoyed _____ the documents. (not, receive)
7 We looked forward _____ you home last year. (have)
8 You forbade me _____ another cigarette. (smoke)
9 Excuse me _____ you earlier. (not, approach)
10 I know _____, but I am not an expert. (type)
11 He suggested _____ the course in statistics. (I, take)

12 I refused _____ to any complaints. (listen)
13 She doesn't approve _____ girls. (I, meet)
14 She's used _____ everything and everybody. (criticize)
15 They are interested _____ a fresh survey. (make)
16 They are keen _____ a referendum. (hold)
17 It's no use _____ to persuade me. (try)
18 He doesn't mind _____ you the new model. (show)
19 They are afraid _____ the police. (involve)
20 Your help will enable _____ all my problems. (I, solve)

Exercise 43 Hope, think, wish

Fill the blank in each of the following sentences with *hope* or *think* or *wish*, without changing the form of the word of your choice in any way.

1 I _____ you would look after the garden.
2 I _____ you eventually receive the gift I have posted to you.
3 I _____ we have met before; wasn't it at the zoo?
4 They say they _____ I hadn't gone away; they are feeling so lonely.
5 I _____ you must have got the wrong person.
6 I _____ you well; come and see us soon.
7 I _____ you haven't injured yourself; that was a big drop.
8 Do whatever you _____ fit.
9 To _____ a lot about one's problems may not be the best way to solve them.
10 I _____ you get better soon.

Exercise 44 Verbs in common idioms

Fill the blank in each of the following sentences with one of these verbs; *make, do, take, come, catch, fall, go, fly*. The form of the verb should be varied as the sentence requires.

1 I added up the figures: they _____ to 980.
2 She _____ sick last week.

3 He would _____ to any lengths to help a friend.
4 He _____ a complete fool of himself last night.
5 Whatever you _____, don't invite him here again.
6 She has _____ in love with an Army Officer.
7 You must _____ every effort to trace the owner of this car.
8 Will you _____ me a favour, and put some stamps on this letter?
9 The play _____ well; there was a lot of applause at the end.
10 The renewal of your licence _____ next week.
11 They hope to _____ a success of their marriage after all.
12 It has _____ to my notice that you were absent all last week.
13 You will _____ yourself an injury if you keep trying to carry heavy things.
14 He is sadistic; he _____ pleasure in tormenting people.
15 I spoke to her but she had already _____ asleep.
16 It will _____ much for your prestige if you can attend in person.
17 She _____ into a rage when I told her to guard her tongue.
18 It _____ all sorts to make a world.
19 If I _____ you eating again, you will get nothing tomorrow.
20 It _____ me five hours yesterday to do only twenty kilometres.
21 It was crazy – the door-knob _____ off in my hand.
22 There was no food to be had, so we all _____ hungry.
23 I shall _____ mad if I don't hear from my brother soon.
24 He _____ pains to ensure that I arrived at my destination.
25 How time _____! It's already five o'clock.
26 He wants to _____ inquiries about the times of departures.
27 This proposal has _____ a mockery of all our long-held policies.

28 How does that tune _____? I have forgotten it.
29 She _____ something very surprising last night by seizing the keys.
30 You will _____ cold if you don't put on a sweater.

Exercise 45 Lexis: various items

Choose a word from the list at the top to fill the blank in each of the sentences underneath. Do not use any word more than once. Not all the words in the list will be used.

liking march remind seized repaired size support convince ignored left forgot shaved letters borrow rampant side persuade room neglected dresses beat remember chance likeness popular cut of tread alphabets maintained fit give up clothes won scraped lend

1 'Many of my _____ are very old,' he said.
2 It is because of his _____ for you that he has made you his deputy.
3 I _____ him twice, but he wouldn't accept defeat.
4 He _____ his radio inside the shop.
5 _____ softly as you enter the house; don't wake them up.
6 He used to have a moustache, but he _____ it off last week.
7 They _____ trying to communicate with him.
8 Ignorance about the way to treat this disease is _____.
9 The king _____ demands that he should retreat.
10 How many _____ does the word 'civilization' contain?
11 What is the amount you want me to _____ you?
12 I will _____ her to speak to her husband on your behalf.
13 Your generator has been well _____, which is why it has never given trouble.
14 'This is the exact _____ of my mother,' I said to the artist.
15 There is no _____ left on this boat; try another one.
16 They've _____ the electricity, and we don't know when we shall get it back again.

17 I am going to sign them, but _____ me again tomorrow.
18 We _____ the team that is going to win, of course.
19 These shoes are not really my _____; bring out a 42.
20 I wanted to interview you today, but I didn't have the
_____.

Exercise 46 *Words confused because of similar sound*

Choose one of the words in brackets to complete each of the
following sentences:

1 When they achieved (independent, independence) they
joined the United Nations.
2 In (other, order) to give his dependents better security, he
took out a life insurance policy.
3 We (taught, thought) you would never succeed.
4 They were ordered to (match, march) as far as the next
ridge.
5 He (lives, leaves) very simply, and never drinks or smokes.
6 He (owes, owns) a large fleet of lorries.
7 If you (lose, loose) this card, we certainly cannot give you
another one.
8 They left him to his (fate, faith), and he perished soon
afterwards.
9 They will (cease, seize) to grumble once they are satisfied.
10 The (prize, price) paid for their victory was severe economic
difficulties.
11 We will keep a (sit, seat) vacant in case you turn up.
12 I often (heard, had) it said that you were a genius.
13 No conscientious person likes to be interrupted in the
(course, cause) of duty.
14 If you were ever (giving, given) a free television, would you
refuse it?
15 He was posted there to (guard, guide) the gate.
16 She had to (pack, park) her belongings in great haste and
catch the next train home.
17 His (belief, believe) is that perception does not guarantee
knowledge.

18 (Safe, Save) enough money, and you will soon be able to buy a Honda.
19 The vehicle was (stationary, stationery).
20 The (proof, prove) of what you say lies in this letter.

Exercise 47 Be, been, being

Fill the blank in each of the following sentences with *be* or *been* or *being*:

1 _____ certain that she was in agony, I took her to hospital.
2 It has never _____ my intention to deceive you.
3 They were _____ held in custody.
4 He was accused of _____ an accomplice of the gang.
5 It used to _____ said that the world was flat.
6 Don't _____ daft! He is your brother.
7 The cry may have _____ that of a jackal.
8 The message is even now _____ shown on their screens.
9 They are about to _____ ferried across the river.
10 He was relieved of the responsibility, _____ quite incompetent.

Exercise 48 Spelling of verb forms

Fill the blank in each of the following sentences with the correct form of the verb in brackets:

1 He was _____ to meet her. (hope)
2 She was _____ a cup of water. (sip)
3 You are not _____ to remain here. (permit)
4 The bird was _____ from one branch to another. (hop)
5 She _____ the two pieces of paper together and gave them to me. (gum)
6 He was _____ off in the direction of the canteen. (stride)
7 I was _____ to hear of your child's death. (stun)
8 The hearings will be _____ next week. (resume)
9 The car _____, but I managed to stop it. (skid)
10 He _____ the boy on the head and said how brave he had been. (pat)

Exercise 49 Punctuation

Each of the following items contains errors of punctuation. Rewrite each correctly.

1 Although I don't know your name; I have seen you before.
2 Who do you think you are? she asked.
3 He said that 'a man without a wife is like a kitchen without a knife'.
4 Thanks to your intervention. We rescued him in time.
5 Please take your bill to the "Pay Office".
6 The western Sudan was seriously affected by drought.
7 Madagascar lies in the Indian Ocean, it is a very large island.
8 Abraham Lincoln lived from 1809–1865.
9 She bought beans maize and rice.
10 You can go now. Though you haven't yet finished the work I gave you.

Exercise 50 General correction exercise

Each of the following sentences contains ONE mistake – a wrong ending, a word misplaced, a misspelling, etc. Rewrite the sentences correctly, but be careful to change only what must be changed to make each sentence correct. Do not change what is correct already.

Example 1 He speak with a strange accent.
Correction: He speaks with a strange accent.
Example 2 He asked us what were our names.
Correction: He asked us what our names were.

The mistake in Example 2 is correctly identified as the wrong order of the words 'were our names'. That is all that *must* be changed. There is no need to change the tense used in the sentence from past to present, for example. Of course, 'He asks us what our names are' would be a correct sentence in an appropriate context, but here to put 'asks' would amount to over-correction.

1 This test is difficult than the one we had last week.

2 I wouldn't take up needlework if I were you; your eyes are not enough sharp.

3 Instead of him to ask us for tickets, the gatekeeper let both of us in free.

4 She speaks German language like a native.

5 I was most greatful to receive such a large donation from you.

6 You will be responsible for the maintainance of your own sections.

7 The visitors they were seeking information about our in-service courses.

8 I was annoyed with her because he did not wish to speak to me.

9 She has always jealoused her younger sister, who is actually the more intelligent of the two.

10 He used three weeks in his home town before travelling down to Warri.

11 'Am very happy to write and tell you that I have passed my exams with flying colours.

12 Is very surprising to hear that he has once again broken his ankle.

13 She turned deaf ears to all our pleadings on behalf of young Okeke.

14 There were plenty witnesses of the incident, so be careful what you say.

15 She was young and beautiful, she was well-educated, she had a generally sweet personality; all these told me she was the one for me.

16 If I am chanced, I will attend the party with you.

17 May you kindly leave my house this minute, and never come back?

18 He's the best lawyer we have, and I advise you to avail his services.

19 He is used to offing his hat whenever he enters a church.

20 I went to the clinic to remove the plaster from my leg.

21 Everything else has been attended to; it remains only the problem of lighting.

22 These tablets will enable you sleep better than at present.

23 He use to go walking with his dog very early every morning.

24 The climate at this altitude is very conducive.

25 He gave you a wonderful testimonial; even, he phoned your headmaster and spoke to him personally.

26 A: 'Would you like another beer?' B: 'No, please, I've had enough.'

27 That programme we watched last night was extremely very enjoyable.

28 That girl you have been inquiring about answers Elizabeth.

29 I searched through all my papers, but the birth certificate was not among.

30 If you meet him absent, come and tell me and we will try to contact him at home.

31 I have not been opportuned so far this year to make a trip to Lagos.

32 I shall be very annoyed if he tries to tamper any of our arrangements.

33 Conclusively, let us in the remaining minutes examine the problems of diabetics.

34 I do not quite follow your arguement; could you repeat that statement?

35 A huge crowd had gathered; it was a very important occassion.

36 I doubt if he will do well in academics; he should go into business at once.

37 We are not surprised he has come late; after all, he always disappoints in one way or another.

38 Only James had learned his part thoroughly; the rest actors had a long way to go.

39 I cannot continue with this work; there is no carbon paper again.

40 A large trailer was coming up at top speed at my back.

41 I can't see clearly at my front; the wipers seem to have stopped.

42 I had paid my deposit, but there hadn't yet released the radio.

43 The exchanging of thatch for metal roofs has now become rampant in the villages.

44 They refused to resume work until they might have taken their midday meal.
45 He became an Islamic in 1945.
46 He was driving along the road when he came to one river, overshadowed by a huge tree.
47 Some people spend their entire lifes unable to decide what they really want to do.
48 The Admiral assembled his fleets and began the bombardment.
49 He sailed down the Nile as far as the Cairo.
50 Help me call the storekeeper; he is wanted by the Chief Accountant.

Answer Key

Exercise 1

1 people 2 sheep 3 trousers 4 rallies 5 theses 6 bonus
7 data 8 heroes 9 radius 10 series 11 cargoes 12 news
13 medium 14 thieves 15 beliefs

Exercise 2

1 damage 2 armies 3 Executive 4 people 5 issue 6 funds
7 élite 8 delay 9 depressions 10 weight 11 alphabet
12 enemy 13 advice 14 restrictions 15 weights 16 sports
17 gossip 18 property 19 depression 20 damages

Exercise 3

1 instruction 2 shirt 3 dialect 4 scene 5 permit 6 an
examination 7 practice 8 load 9 hands 10 loan 11 joke
12 harvest 13 meal 14 letter 15 rebuke 16 job 17 novel
18 currency 19 rumour 20 honour

Exercise 4

1 wars 2 sugars 3 foam 4 beards 5 scholarships 6 styles
7 paint 8 behaviour 9 position 10 soap

Exercise 5

1 belongings 2 washing 3 failings 4 shooting 5 savings
6 hearing 7 feelings 8 surroundings 9 cuttings 10 greetings

Exercise 6

1 They have installed new equipment. 2 The soldiers put on their
armour. 3 They like to wear jewellery. 4 They have repaired all
the machinery. 5 They stick to their beliefs. 6 They put some
sugar in their cups. 7 They entered into correspondence with the
lecturers. 8 They had their dresses mended. 9 They provided
the information required of them. 10 They like comfortable
furniture. 11 The houses lack good plumbing. 12 The companies
want to employ more staff. 13 They were accused of
manslaughter. 14 They dropped their opposition to the plans.

15 They often listen to music. 16 Their positions had been carefully chosen. 17 They acted out of revenge. 18 They did harm to themselves. 19 Our sons are looking for work. 20 Your friends are soon going to obtain their degrees.

Exercise 7

1 He was ironing his trousers. 2 He did not know my whereabouts. 3 He cannot see properly when he removes his spectacles. 4 He stamped my passport. 5 This animal has a long tail. 6 A world power has a large fleet. 7 He lives in the best quarters in the camp. 8 The roof was covered with asbestos. 9 I was asked to buy fresh equipment. 10 This species of spider is found in North America.

She may be used instead of 'he', and 'her' instead of 'his'.

Exercise 8

1 Criminals   2 unemployed   3 deaf   4 blind   5 nomads
6 British   7 German   8 innocent   9 unsuitable   10 rich
11 particulars   12 good   13 poor   14 subject   15 junior
16 dead   17 alcoholics   18 goods   19 infant   20 elderly

Exercise 9

1 I spoke to the Manager's secretary. 2 She saw the State Governor. 3 (no change) 4 I went to my friend's funeral. 5 I wrote down the account number. 6 I passed through the College gates. 7 I reached the mountain top. 8 She was a thriller writer. 9 The treasure lay on the ocean bed. 10 I entered the factory precincts. 11 I visited the Army headquarters. 12 He went for a five-mile walk. 13 A traffic policeman's job looks very tedious. 14 Man belongs to the animal kingdom. 15 (no change) 16 She sat down in the University library. 17 (no change) 18 We are looking for a fifty-year-old vehicle. 19 (no change) 20 Building construction can be a profitable business.

Exercise 10

The correct words to fill the gaps are as follows:
1 –   2 a   3 an   4 –   5 –   6 –   7 a   8 –   9 an   10 –   11 a
12 a   13 –   14 a   15 an   16 –   17 a   18 –   19 –   20 a

Exercise 11

1 The   2 the   3 –   4 the   5 –   6 –   7 –   8 The   9 –   10 –
11 –   12 –   13 –   14 –   15 –   16 –   17 –   18 The   19 the
20 –

Exercise 12
1 the   2 the   3 –   4 –   5 the   6 –   7 the   8 –   9 The   10 –
11 the   12 –   13 the   14 –   15 –   16 The   17 The   18 The
19 the   20 the

Exercise 13
1 a   2 a   3 –   4 –   5 –   6 an   7 –   8 The   9 the   10 –

Exercise 14
1 d   2 b   3 a   4 b   5 b   6 c   7 a   8 c   9 a   10 d

Exercise 15
A 1 all my   2 A whole   3 either/those   4 Five *or* Many/ours
5 Many other *or* Five other
B 1 Most/few   2 every two/three   3 a   4 any/some   5 None/our
C 1 All the   2 a whole   3 Much/this   4 several/any
5 more/another
D 1 Half/that   2 their next   3 Neither/those   4 Much/many
5 Some more

Exercise 16
1 c   2 a   3 b   4 c   5 b   6 b   7 c   8 b   9 b   10 d

Exercise 17
1 I have a friend called Johnson who walks 5 miles every day.
2 The things belonged to a shepherd whose whereabouts were
unknown.   3 She left him for her boy-friend, which did not
surprise us.   4 I have come with a spanner which you can use to
tighten the bolts.   5 There were riots also in Kassani, of which we
have so far received few details.   6 All the things you left *or* which
you left *or* that you left in your room are going to be carried away
and either sold or burned.   7 The landlady, whose instructions had
been ignored, stood on the stairs and shouted.   8 We must now go
and call on Mr Matatu, who saved your brother's life *or* thanks to
whom your brother's life was saved.   9 I have found the bunch of
keys (which/that) you said you were looking for.   10 He stood under
the tree in which according to local belief a spirit dwelt.

Exercise 18
1 is making   2 belongs   3 is sleeping   4 is shining   5 has   6 fly
7 seems   8 contains   9 reach   10 see

Exercise 19
1 flew   2 let   3 forbade   4 cut   5 spent   6 split   7 shed   8 lit
9 met   10 shut

277

Exercise 20

1 crept 2 chosen 3 have now hidden 4 has just driven 5 cast
6 put 7 swollen 8 struck 9 knelt 10 had already risen

Exercise 21

1 Do 2 isn't 3 has 4 didn't 5 does 6 doesn't 7 were
8 weren't 9 didn't 10 Were *or* Weren't 11 Do *or* Dont't
12 Are 13 have 14 was 15 had 16 don't 17 did 18 Is
19 aren't 20 don't 21 Has 22 wasn't 23 Hasn't 24 Did
25 do

Exercise 22

1 doesn't he 2 can they 3 do we 4 won't they 5 would she
6 didn't I 7 didn't he 8 is it 9 aren't they 10 wasn't it
11 weren't we 12 will you 13 won't you 14 hasn't he 15 isn't
it 16 doesn't it 17 have you 18 wouldn't he 19 does he
20 aren't they

Exercise 23

1 b 2 d 3 d 4 b 5 c 6 a 7 b 8 d 9 b 10 a 11 b
12 a 13 d 14 c 15 d 16 b 17 e 18 c 19 a 20 c

Exercise 24

1 had already gone 2 had often seen 3 have now received *or* will
now have received 4 has been explained 5 had collapsed 6 has
been having 7 had made 8 have asked 9 received 10 had
been defeated 11 has just been made 12 had really said 13 has
been reading 14 has happened 15 had been falling 16 had just
arrived 17 have ever been insulted 18 has been feeling 19 had
been done 20 have gone

Exercise 25

has *or* have released told were still expected would not be
were announced had succeeded was first reported added was
now preparing *or* were now preparing

Exercise 26

1 The seeds are blown about by the wind. 2 The scene was filmed
(by our cameramen). 3 This road has been closed to traffic (by
them). 4 He was surprised that the locusts had returned. 5 All
restrictions will be abolished (by them). 6 You are often seen
walking in the rain (by people). 7 A fresh census will be
conducted (by them). 8 A solution to this growing problem is
being sought (by us). 9 I was being kept in a dark cell (by them).

10 Anyone they catch is likely to be charged with fraud.   11 The
loss was reported to the authorities (by him).   12 The bell was
rung (by Helen).   13 Your words must be spoken in a whisper.
14 One of our ships was sunk (by them).   15 Three of the
conspirators are being shot at dawn tomorrow (by them).
16 Science subjects were not being taught any more (by them).
17 This cloth is woven on a traditional type of loom (by them).
18 We are pleased to get letters from you.   19 Some papers had
been thrust into a pigeon-hole (by him).   20 If this round is won
by Amaka, the victory will be ours.

Exercise 27
1 Is situated   2 is comprised   3 consists   4 is held   5 is believed
6 is wounded   7 refer   8 be held   9 be referred   10 stops

Exercise 28
1 a   2 c   3 d   4 d   5 a   6 d   7 c   8 a   9 c   10 d   11 d
12 a   13 b   14 d   15 b   16 b   17 a   18 c   19 a   20 e

Exercise 29
1 will   2 would   3 would   4 will   5 will   6 will   7 will   8 will
9 would   10 would

Exercise 30
1 a   2 d   3 c   4 a   5 d   6 d   7 b   8 b   9 b   10 d

Exercise 31
1 in   2 By   3 in   4 in   5 at   6 By   7 at   8 in   9 on   10 by

Exercise 32
1 With   2 with   3 For   4 from   5 to or up to or as far as   6 out
of   7 under   8 in front of   9 with   10 at

Exercise 33
1 in   2 on   3 On   4 at   5 on   6 in   7 at   8 On   9 At   10 in
11 in   12 in   13 with   14 in   15 on   16 in   17 With   18 in
19 in   20 in

Exercise 34
1 whole   2 light   3 way   4 attempt   5 odds   6 times   7 course
8 time   9 impression   10 board   11 level   12 confidence
13 cause   14 opinion   15 way   16 context   17 confidence
18 time   19 attempt   20 course

Exercise 35
1 a   2 d   3 c   4 d   5 a   6 d   7 b   8 c   9 c   10 a   11 b

Exercise 36
1 angrily 2 bad 3 sour 4 sharply 5 stupid 6 delicious
7 hard 8 eagerly 9 likely 10 carefully 11 hardly 12 clear
13 exciting 14 badly 15 fast

Exercise 37
1 so 2 too 3 enough 4 very 5 somehow 6 very 7 rather *or*
very *or* too 8 so 9 so much 10 very much *or* rather 11 too
12 somehow 13 so much 14 very much 15 Rather

Exercise 38
1 – 2 more 3 more 4 – 5 more 6 – 7 – 8 more 9 more
10 –

Exercise 39
1 c 2 b 3 d 4 b 5 a 6 d 7 c 8 c 9 d 10 d

Exercise 40
The correct words to fill the blanks are as follows:
1 – 2 – 3 up 4 up 5 back 6 – 7 up 8 – 9 back 10 –
11 – 12 up 13 – 14 back 15 up

Exercise 41
1 for 2 – 3 on 4 of 5 – 6 on 7 with 8 – 9 for
10 with 11 – 12 in 13 – 14 for 15 on 16 on 17 with
18 of 19 of 20 – 21 on 22 for 23 with 24 of 25 –

Exercise 42
1 on reading 2 to having 3 not finding 4 to light 5 to hear
6 not to receive 7 to having 8 to smoke 9 for not approaching
10 how to type 11 that I took *or* my taking 12 to listen 13 of
my meeting *or* of me meeting 14 to criticizing 15 in making
16 on holding 17 trying 18 showing 19 of involving 20 me to
solve

Exercise 43
1 wish 2 hope 3 think 4 wish 5 think 6 wish 7 hope
8 think 9 think 10 hope

Exercise 44
1 came 2 fell 3 go 4 made 5 do 6 fallen 7 make 8 do
9 went 10 falls 11 make 12 come 13 do 14 takes 15 fallen
16 do 17 flew 18 takes 19 catch 20 took 21 came 22 went
23 go 24 took 25 flies 26 make 27 made 28 go 29 did
30 catch

Exercise 45

1 clothes 2 liking 3 beat 4 left 5 Tread 6 shaved
7 remember 8 rampant 9 ignored 10 letters 11 lend
12 persuade 13 maintained 14 likeness 15 room 16 cut off
17 remind 18 support 19 size 20 chance

Exercise 46

1 independence 2 order 3 thought 4 march 5 lives 6 owns
7 lose 8 fate 9 cease 10 price 11 seat 12 heard 13 course
14 given 15 guard 16 pack 17 belief 18 Save 19 stationary
20 proof

Exercise 47

1 Being 2 been 3 being 4 being 5 be 6 be 7 been
8 being 9 be 10 being

Exercise 48

1 hoping 2 sipping 3 permitted 4 hopping 5 gummed
6 striding 7 stunned 8 resumed 9 skidded 10 patted

Exercise 49

1 Although I don't know your name, I have seen you before.
2 'Who do you think you are?' she asked. 3 He said that a man
without a wife is like a kitchen without a knife. 4 Thanks to your
intervention we rescued him in time. 5 Please take your bill to the
Pay Office. 6 The Western Sudan was seriously affected by
drought. 7 Madagascar lies in the Indian Ocean. It is a very large
island. 8 Abraham Lincoln lived from 1809 to 1865. 9 She
bought beans, maize, and rice. 10 You can go now, though you
haven't yet finished the work I gave you.

Exercise 50

1 This test is more difficult than the one we had last week. 2 I
wouldn't take up needlework if I were you; your eyes are not sharp
enough. 3 Instead of asking us for tickets, the gatekeeper let both
of us in free. 4 She speaks German like a native. 5 I was most
grateful to receive such a large donation from you. 6 You will be
responsible for the maintenance of your own sections. 7 The
visitors were seeking information about our in-service courses. 8 I
was annoyed with her because she did not wish to speak to me.
9 She has always been jealous of her younger sister, who is actually
the more intelligent of the two. 10 He spent three weeks in his
home town before travelling down to Warri. 11 I am *or* I'm very
happy to write and tell you that I have passed my exams with flying

colours.   12 It is *or* It's very surprising to hear that he has once again broken his ankle.   13 She turned a deaf ear to all our pleadings on behalf of young Okeke.   14 There were plenty of witnesses of the incident, so be careful what you say.   15 She was young and beautiful, she was well-educated, she had a generally sweet personality; all this told me she was the one for me.   16 If I have the chance, I will attend the party with you.   17 Will you kindly leave my house this minute, and never come back?   18 He's the best lawyer we have, and I advise you to use *or* make use of *or* avail yourself of his services.   19 He is used to taking off his hat whenever he enters a church.   20 I went to the clinic to have the plaster removed from my leg.   21 Everything else has been attended to; only the problem of lighting remains.   22 These tablets will enable you to sleep better than at present.   23 He used to go walking with his dog very early every morning.   24 The climate at this altitude is very agreeable.   25 He gave you a wonderful testimonial; he even phoned your headmaster and spoke to him personally.   26 A: 'Would you like another beer?' B: 'No, thank you, I've had enough.'   27 That programme we watched last night was extremely enjoyable.   28 That girl you have been enquiring about is called Elizabeth.   29 I searched through all my papers, but the birth certificate was not among them. 30 If you find him absent, come and tell me and we will try to contact him at home.   31 I have not had the opportunity so far this year to go to Lagos.   32 I shall be very annoyed if he tries to tamper with any of our arrangements.   33 Finally, let us in the remaining minutes examine the problems of diabetics.   34 I do not quite follow your argument; could you repeat that statement?   35 A huge crowd had gathered; it was a very important occasion.   36 I doubt if he will do well in the academic field; he should go into business at once. 37 We are not surprised he has come late; after all he always disappoints us in one way or another.   38 Only James had learned his part thoroughly; the other actors had a long way to go.   39 I cannot continue with this work; there is no more carbon paper *or* no carbon paper left.   40 A large trailer was coming up at top speed behind me. 41 I can't see clearly in front of me; the wipers seem to have stopped.   42 I had paid my deposit, but they hadn't yet released the radio.   43 The exchanging of thatch for metal roofs has now become widespread in the villages.   44 They refused to resume work until they had taken their midday meal.   45 He became a Muslim *or* Moslem in 1945.   46 He was driving along the road when he came to a river, overshadowed by a huge tree.   47 Some people spend their entire lives unable to decide what they really want to do.   48 The Admiral assembled his fleet and began the bombardment.   49 He sailed down the Nile as far as Cairo.   50 Please call the storekeeper; he is wanted by the Chief Accountant.

Index

Numbers refer to the items listed in Chapters 1–15. Abbreviations used in the index:
w.u. wrongly used
w.o. wrongly omitted
w.f. wrongly followed
w.sp. wrongly spelled
w.pr. wrongly pronounced

285